I0820292

About Island Press

Since 1984, the nonprofit organization Island Press has been stimulating, shaping, and communicating ideas that are essential for solving environmental problems worldwide. With more than 1,000 titles in print and some 30 new releases each year, we are the nation's leading publisher on environmental issues. We identify innovative thinkers and emerging trends in the environmental field. We work with world-renowned experts and authors to develop cross-disciplinary solutions to environmental challenges.

Island Press designs and executes educational campaigns, in conjunction with our authors, to communicate their critical messages in print, in person, and online using the latest technologies, innovative programs, and the media. Our goal is to reach targeted audiences—scientists, policy makers, environmental advocates, urban planners, the media, and concerned citizens—with information that can be used to create the framework for long-term ecological health and human well-being.

Island Press gratefully acknowledges major support from The Bobolink Foundation, The Curtis and Edith Munson Foundation, The Forrest C. and Frances H. Lattner Foundation, The Freedom Together Foundation, The Kresge Foundation, The Summit Charitable Foundation, Inc., and many other generous organizations and individuals.

PRESERVING with PURPOSE

PRESERVING with PURPOSE

REIMAGINING BUILDINGS FOR COMMUNITY BENEFIT

AMY HETLETVEDT

Library of Congress Control Number: 2025934649

All Island Press books are printed on environmentally responsible materials.

Manufactured in the United States of America
10 9 8 7 6 5 4 3 2 1

Keywords: abandoned building, adaptive reuse, architecture, beneficial preservation, blight, building conservation, community participation, disinvestment, endangered building, historic preservation, historic property, incremental development, lower-budget preservation, poetic intervention, population decline, practical intervention, priority intervention, temporary use, threatened building, vacant property

This book is dedicated
to my beloved father,
who, during its writing,
left this world for his
final and complete
restoration.

CONTENTS

Classic car tail light detail, 2009. (Library of Congress, Prints & Photographs Division, photo by Carol M. Highsmith [LC-DIG-highsm-04405])

Preface

> "I never considered myself a great architect. I'm more of a creative problem solver with good taste and a soft spot for logistical nightmares."
>
> —Maria Semple, *Where'd You Go, Bernadette*

I thought it was a hearse I was looking at.

We pulled up to the old Redford Theater on Detroit's West Side. It was the early 2000s—at the end of the thirty years or so that the world had forgotten about Detroit, the decades in which it existed outside of time, in its own orbit, and the gaze of the world was still turned away. There was a force field, an invisible line around its borders, and what went on inside was isolated, a world within itself.

This is not to say that it wasn't influenced by larger socioeconomic forces, but for those decades, which encapsulated the twenty-year tenure of Mayor Coleman Young, the outside world left Detroit alone.

It was the major criticism I had of my architectural education in nearby Ann Arbor. Not once did I have a studio project that engaged with this urban metropolis 40 miles away. I was assigned design studies like a loft for a violin maker, a bridge in an Olympic village, a rural retreat for an artistic couple, and although my design abilities progressed through these exercises, I wondered what sort of architects this education was preparing us to be.

As a provocative project for a class in my third year at university, I created an installation that hung on the wall outside the administration corridor of the architecture school. *I am home(less) un(less)* was a series of black boards with stark white text. Each board was hinged and opened with a salvaged metal cabinet handle. The handles invited passersby to lift them up and peek into reflective statements about their present, their future, and their relationship with the other. Who exactly were we becoming? Who were our clients? What did our own choices—both in life and in vocation—mean for others and the world around us?

I have no way of measuring this installation's effect except on myself.

After a stint on the West Coast, completing graduate school and working in the urban context of a thriving tech-boom economy, my husband and I moved to Detroit. We settled into a brick Tudor in an East Side neighborhood during a time in which it was a statistical anomaly for a White person to be moving *into* Detroit.

Early in those years, we found ourselves on one summer evening pulling up outside the Redford Theater. It was one of the few neighborhood theaters still open in Detroit, the anchor of a one-story brick commercial strip. Operated by the Motor City Theater Organ Society, the Redford still had its working pipe organ, and the live prelude and postlude were the sound spectacles that had drawn us there.

But outside was an even more fantastical prelude. Underneath the hulking cantilever of the marquee, what appeared to me as a hearse was parked in front of the theater, a '60s machine, long and low, a chariot of luxury and dignity—except that it had been modified to look like the Ectomobile from the 1980s movie *Ghostbusters*.

It had bullhorns mounted on the hood. A siren on its roof gleamed in the low evening light. And emblazoned across the side of the front door was the slogan "Motor City Blight Busters."

I loved this vehicle immediately. Its rich symbolism: an automobile as the savior for the Motor City! I loved it for its cheekiness. And I loved it for all the questions that it brought to my mind.

How exactly were they busting blight with this fantastic machine? What did they store in its cavernous back end? Was it equipment to take down? (I envisioned sledgehammers, crowbars, explosives?) Or was it equipment to build up?

Furthermore, what was blight?

Was it a physical condition of deterioration? Or was it socio-psychological, like a collective feeling of hopelessness?

How would this outlandish machine fight hopelessness? When you opened up the rear door, would a bunch of balloons crowd out and lift up to the sky? Maybe a cannon shooting out encouraging messages like backfires from its tailpipe?[1]

Much was crowded into our decade in the city after we encountered the Blight Mobile. I grew and learned from the experience of living in a community where I was a racial minority. We joined the neighborhood association, which cooperatively funded, for example, the snow plowing of side streets that the city did not provide. We ran up against challenges that were common to all residents of the city at that time, daily frustrations and inconveniences of living in a place where systems were breaking down or broken. The public lighting system was a disaster, the city was pronounced a food desert,[2] and the emergency network was stretched to its limit.

I learned professional lessons from practicing architecture in Detroit and in my time serving on the city's Historic District Commission. I participated in difficult decisions, meeting with countless situations where an owner's means could not keep pace with a building's needs and others where an owner saw their historic building not as an asset but as a nuisance or obstacle.

As metal theft continued to rise aggressively,[3] our state-based preservation network advocated for stronger scrap yard monitoring and accountability. Many church clients had their flashings and gutters stolen. Flashings and downspouts are necessary, but continuous replacement was demoralizing. They'd rather have spent their money on other things. (As I would have when my car's catalytic converter was sawn off in a church parking lot.)

The ten years that we lived in Detroit were the longest I've lived anywhere. And in the ten plus years since then I've continued pursuing the questions I began asking there about buildings, about blight—about disinvestment, demolition, and the metaphysical chasm between ruin and restoration.

The ideas in this book are built on my own experiences and those of many others. In my personal and professional journey, I've learned from the work and writings of community activists such as Dr. John Perkins, architects such as Samuel Mockbee, and artists such as Sister Corita Kent. I'm inspired by neighbors and friends in Detroit and people I've met who are living and working in disinvested contexts and caring for buildings all over the world.

Although my own life has been itinerant, I admire the character and persistence of those who have remained firmly rooted in place and community.

Great Architecture with a capital "A" has never been, for me, the primary interest or the end goal. Logistical nightmares need champions. Problems need thinkers and riskers. Complexity invites us further in. Entering into complexity demands something of our intellect and imagination as we begin to unravel causality and envision solutions. But it demands something of our hearts as well: conviction and compassion.

During the writing of this book, I sat down with John George, founder of Detroit Blight Busters, on a snowy morning in the busy café started by Blight Busters on Detroit's Northwest Side.

Of course, I asked about the Blight Mobile. "So, what kind of car was that thing? Was it a hearse?"

"Naw. It wasn't a hearse. It was a turquoise station wagon that had been used as an ambulance."[4]

Funny, a vehicle that for the last twenty years in my mind has been a conveyance for the dead was actually an ambulance to assist the living. This revelation was a clarion call for me: So-called blight is best addressed not with a hearse but with healing.

Whether you're an architect who has been invited to work in a disinvested community, a resident, activist, or artist engaging with existing buildings, or someone who is simply drawn to think more deeply about the *why* of vacant, abandoned, and distressed buildings and *what* we can do about it, I invite you in. I invite you to enter into this conversation with your whole person.

In the topsy-turvy world of *Alice's Adventures in Wonderland*, created by Lewis Carroll, Alice asks the enigmatic Cheshire Cat, "Would you tell me, please, which way I ought to go from here?" He replies, "That depends a good deal on where you want to get to."[5] This book is not a recipe or a roadmap but an open discussion on how, together, we can incrementally change course.

In this collage, reptiles inhabit the spaces that humans have left behind while the figure outside the door kneels to peek in. Do we, together as humans, dare be invited back into the process of creation within the wreckage we've made of Eden? (*Guests in an Abandoned House*, circa twentieth century CE. Collage, paper. 34.6 × 39.9 cm. inv no. AM1981-160. Photo by Audrey Laurans. Artist: Adolf Hoffmeister [1902–1973], Czech painter. Location: Centre Georges Pompidou/Paris/France. Digital Image © CNAC/MNAM, Dist. RMN-Grand Palais/Art Resource, New York, NY)

Introduction

> "Years of experience, much of it forged in the crucible of misguided programs such as urban renewal, have clearly demonstrated the folly of destroying a place in order to save it."
>
> —Richard Moe, *Rebuilding Community*

One of the most sustainable things we can do at a societal scale is to invest in existing communities, making use of the embodied energy of generations before us. Yet investment flows into developing greenfields further and further from our historic city centers and in thick blankets around rural towns, leaving core communities more vulnerable and underresourced.

A slow drive down Lafayette Avenue on the South Side of Chicago in 2019 reveals a streetscape not so different from other disinvested Rust Belt communities, with empty lots and abandoned or distressed buildings. Some of the remaining buildings are neatly kept, trying to hold it together. Vacancy characterizes much of the neighborhood.

The density of this neighborhood in 2019 is perhaps not so different from what it was in 1870, when John Raber chose it for building a brick Italianate residence on 6 acres. Now, the landmarked Raber residence is almost completely obscured by tree growth and vines, its boarded windows rendering its tall façade expressionless. Further down the block, a twentieth-century brick building, formerly the home of the Mount Mariah Missionary Baptist Church and Deliverance Healing Temple, is also vacant, its windows filled with wavy glass blocks. On the half-dozen lots between them, the only structure that remains is a single-story bungalow from the 1960s, its picture window embellished with white shutters and a single trimmed shrub. Around this home, a chain-link fence defines its island.

The Raber House in Chicago in 1999. (Photo by Camilo José Vergara. Raber House, 5670 S. Lafayette Ave., Chicago, 1999. Library of Congress, Prints & Photographs Division [reproduction number LC-DIG-vrg-09604])

“After generations of municipal neglect, predatory lending practices, and increased waves of foreclosure, the neighborhood was hollowed out and its structures demolished,” Sweet Water Foundation details.[1]

“Compounded by several decades of loss of population . . . the area sat vacant, ‘blighted,’ and deeply scarred” by what Sweet Water Foundation describes as a “constructed ecology of absence,” explains Anthony Balas in a Mellon Foundation publication of their interview.[2]

This constructed ecology includes the built environment, part of our whole Earth ecosystem. In disinvested communities, the deep effects of absence are visible within the constructed ecology. There is a marked vacancy and lack of investment to fully address the properties that remain.

Much of the direct demolition of the built fabric in urban communities in the United States took place through federal programs: so-called slum clearings beginning in the 1930s and urban renewal and transportation planning projects of the 1950s and 1960s. Many urban freeway construction projects during these decades reinforced inequalities by destroying or isolating lower-income neighborhoods while providing a convenient conduit for those with the means and opportunity to work in the city but live in the suburbs.[3] Essentially, these large-scale transportation projects aided in draining the cities. Generational wealth, economic stability, and deep sociocultural connections were affected, and the effects continue to be felt in these communities today.

The preservation movement in the United States gained traction in the 1960s, sparked by the demolition of Pennsylvania Station in New York City in 1963. Yet as Richard Moe, former president of the National Trust for Historic Preservation, points out, the nascent decades of the preservation movement in the United States were also the tail end of decades in which bulldozers had been blazing through inner-city communities in the name of urban renewal.

“Abandoned buildings can break a neighborhood’s heart,” Moe says. “Demolished buildings can destroy its soul. When disinvestment, poor maintenance and abandonment leave a neighborhood pock marked with vacant or dilapidated buildings, public officials and citizens often seek a quick solution to the community’s woes by razing the deteriorated structures. Demolition may effect a dramatic change in the neighborhood’s appearance, but it’s rarely a change for the better.”[4]

A Works Progress Administration–era poster promoting new housing as a crime deterrent, 1936. (Eliminate Crime in the Slums Through Housing. New York, 1936. Library of Congress, Prints & Photographs Division. New York: Federal Art Project. [LC-DIG-ppmsca-52154])

A sales office for new houses on the outskirts of Detroit, Michigan, 1941. (Library of Congress, Prints & Photographs Division, FSA/OWI Collection [LC-USF34-063667-D]. Photo by John Vachon)

The aesthetic of abandonment deeply affects its residents. Planner Alan Mallach describes how the disinvested environment can reflect a pervasive lack of hope that has deep sociological roots.[5] Abandoned buildings can be a source of physical danger, from unstable building elements to hazardous materials to a harbor for criminal activity. In many ways, abandoned, distressed, and underused buildings are experienced as burdens.

But removing these buildings can also have negative effects. University of Toronto professor of geography and planning Jason Hackworth states that "research affirms some of the concerns being raised by scholars and local officials about past uses of demolition as a stand-alone device, namely, that absent some other form of affirmative development, disinvested neighborhoods do not autonomously revive."[6]

Healthy communities need buildings. In disinvested communities, vacant, abandoned, or deteriorated properties (or VAD properties, as referred to by the Center for Community Progress[7]) are often viewed or experienced as burdens. Yet they also can be reintegrated into an ecosystem of use and serve as reminders of the diverse experiences that have shaped our society.

Disinvested communities, as I define them in this book, are areas that are experiencing or have experienced limited investment and economic activity and are characterized by low property values. The effects of disinvestment include a high incidence of VAD properties. A community can remain in what the Center for Community Progress calls a cycle of systemic vacancy for years, even decades.[8]

In this book I explore how artists, activists, and architects are creatively redeveloping buildings in ways that can be strategic for disinvested communities. Some of these redevelopments offer practical benefits to the community, providing shelter, space for artistic endeavors and creative enterprises, opportunities for teaching and learning, and places for growing food and gathering. Other creative approaches may have a role that is not practical but more poetic or prophetic.

Working in the South Side Chicago neighborhood of the Raber House and Deliverance Healing Temple during its multigenerational harrowing-out (in the words of the Sweet Water Foundation from their interview with Anthony Balas), the Sweet Water Foundation gathered and shared life experiences with neighbors.[9] Soon after acquiring the abandoned church building in 2019, they received a grant from the National Trust to reimagine and revitalize spaces in the community.[10] The foundation proposed focusing community efforts on the church building, renamed the Civic Arts Church, instead of on the Raber House.

The Raber House, which was landmarked by the City of Chicago in 1996, had not found an investor or a new use. The Sweet Water Foundation saw that the nearby abandoned church held different stories and different possibilities for regeneration. Although the church was not landmarked, it was seen as having greater potential to benefit the community as a hub of activity around the arts and its importance in telling certain stories. "The act of preserving and transforming the church . . . will unveil elements of Black History in Chicago that are untold and will reactivate a community asset that is deeply rooted in the history of the people who live in the neighborhood today,"[11] reads a Sweet Water Foundation publication about the project.

As this example demonstrates, although prominent historic buildings can have importance to a community, sometimes buildings that are considered nonhistoric can have equal or greater importance. And, as architect Beth Brant points out in an article for AIA Dallas, reusing so-called nonspecial buildings can have greater sustainability impact than reusing the so-called special ones.[12] Buildings from a broad spectrum of time can be creatively reused to serve purposes that benefit the community.

In *Preserving with Purpose*, I argue for saving buildings that are of value to the community. Whether the building becomes a symbol of resistance, a place of refuge, a teacher, a business incubator, or whether interventions at the site help clean the soil or serve as a marker for mourning or remembrance, good can come to the community through even temporary or partial reuse of an underused site. I believe that widespread demolition removes certain possibilities of goodness without preventing gentrification.

When I talk with people about approaches to the reuse of buildings in disinvested communities, the question that arises most frequently is, "Doesn't this lead to gentrification?"

My response is, "Sometimes." The negative effects of increased investment and raised property values, such as displacement, can occur. Offering discussion in several community profiles about inclusion or affordability as community priorities, I advocate for retaining and building on the physical resources within disinvested communities because, as Alan Mallach points out in his book *The Divided City*, "the reality is that today most neighborhoods that don't revive, go downhill."[13]

A Juneteenth celebration at Civic Arts Church in 2024. The new sliding door on the side of the building activates the open space between the church and the adjacent residential structures, including the Raber House. (Courtesy of Sweet Water Foundation)

In this book, I suggest ways that professionals such as historians, architects, and urban planners who potentially come from outside a disinvested community can participate in a way that respects and empowers community members to consider the best method and use of existing buildings. Part II of this book features examples from around the world of buildings that have been prioritized and strategically preserved by their community for later redevelopment and buildings that have been repurposed or adapted for practical or poetic purposes. This catalog of approaches developed in part because it was a resource that I wished I had in discussions with clients—something to spark the creative process.

Part III offers profiles of four places that were in a cycle of systemic vacancy or at a stage of critical abandonment but have, over time, redeveloped buildings by using the approaches described in this book. Three of these profiles—Project Row Houses in Houston, Texas; The Dorchester Projects and Stony Island Arts Bank in Chicago, Illinois; and Menokin in Warsaw, Virginia—are in the United States. The fourth profile, of 10 Houses on Cairns and the Granby Winter Garden, is in Liverpool, England. Menokin is in a rural area and the others are urban. The examples all have different stories, of course—different ownership models and different dynamics that have played out over time between the individuals and groups involved. Yet in these communities, artists, residents, activists, and architects have approached existing buildings in strategic, creative, purposeful ways.

Although this book is written for a global audience, the perspective is firmly situated in the United States. For example, the book uses the term *preservation* (an Americanism) rather than the term *conservation*, which is more commonly used in other places around the world.[14] I apply global observations to the architecture and preservation fields in the United States because they are the systems in which I was trained and licensed. And because it's my home culture, it's the one with which I am most familiar and feel the most freedom to approach critically.

In addition to discussing the loss of buildings, this book also identifies some barriers to saving them within the disciplines of historic preservation and the building service professions. My goal is not necessarily to revolutionize existing systems but to help make space within them—to create a parenthesis of opportunity—for more buildings in disinvested communities to remain. Architect–preservationist Deborah Burke describes existing buildings as an opportunity "for cities to engage with historical trauma, encourage cultural continuity, and move beyond generic expectations of what older structures can become in a rapidly changing world."[15]

Five years on from a pandemic that underscored our interconnectedness and fragility, we somehow find ourselves more splintered and divided than ever before. We're haunted by persistent social inequities and the urgent ticking of the environmental clock. But when we pause to look around us, we can see afresh the good work that is happening and has already been happening for years, good work that is often overshadowed by higher-budget projects and the insatiable cycle of consumption.

We are no longer in an age (if indeed we ever were) where the Howard Roark archetype of the solitary professional can succeed in addressing the complex issues of our society.[16] We must engage with others not only about how we got to this point but how, together, we can move forward. We can change course away from this constructed ecology of absence and the churning consumption of greenspace toward purposefully preserving environments with existing buildings that are fertile with hope for individual communities and for our planet.

PART I

Addressing the Challenge

Companions in sunsetting limbo: Will it be removal or regeneration? (Erik Olson, *Longtime Neighbors*, oil on canvas, 30 × 40 inches. Courtesy of Erik Olson)

Chapter 1

Why Buildings Are Being Lost: Burdens and Barriers

"What I was going to do would technically be stealing, but from whom? A memory? The people who had abandoned it? The governments that allowed it to fester?"

—Drew Philp, *A $500 House in Detroit: Rebuilding an Abandoned Home and an American City*

The scale of Detroit's depopulation is vast. In the postwar production boom of the 1950s, Detroit reached its peak population of 1.85 million. By 2020, seventy years later, the population had fallen to 640,000, or just slightly over one third its former size.[1] Dispersed over a landmass roughly equivalent in size to Manhattan, San Francisco, and Boston combined, Detroit's remaining population contended with an outsized infrastructure[2] and a slow unraveling of the built environment its resources no longer supported.

Disinvested communities like Detroit are staggering under the economic and psychological burden of vacant, abandoned, and distressed properties. These buildings, their disappearance, and the disinvestment surrounding them are not just inherited problems or a random collision of unfortunate circumstances but the result of socioeconomic forces and deliberate choices.[3]

A policy brief produced for the Vacant Properties Research Network states, "Even though many of the forces and factors responsible for blighted properties are difficult to see, this invisibility does not mean that blighted properties are natural results of urban and suburban development. On the contrary, a number of federal, state, and municipal policies and market trends have helped to create blighted conditions in the U.S. . . . The emergence of blighted properties in shrinking and deindustrializing cities in the U.S. is not happenstance. The emergence of blighted properties is part of a larger pattern of deterioration and neglect."[4]

Disinvestment has a cause, and it also has a cost. In the early 2000s, depopulating Rust Belt cities such as Buffalo, New York, and St. Louis, Missouri, counted more than 30,000 vacant housing units each. The count in Cleveland, Ohio, was 50,000.[5] A 2022 report by the Center for Community Progress states that a conservative estimate of the minimum cost to address vacant and blighted structures in the state of Michigan alone is $1.7 billion. "The direct costs to address these properties," the reports states, "are more than individual communities can bear."[6]

And the costs are more than economic. In his article "How Detroit Became the World Capital of Staring at Abandoned Old Buildings," journalist Mark Binelli recounts Detroiter Marsha Cusic speaking of the "retinal scars" that Detroit's ruined buildings left on children living in the city.[7] Her metaphor left a lasting impression on me. The longer I lived in Detroit, the more I understood how the residual outline of each distressed building was seared into the community's consciousness.

By communities or by owners with more capital resources, historic buildings are being saved. They're being rehabilitated, restored, reused, reinterpreted. Dovecote Studio in Suffolk, England, a steel structure inserted into a partially ruined stone building, is the darling of creative ruins activists. At Bunny Lane House in central New Jersey (United States) architect Adam Kalkin enclosed a nineteenth-century clapboard house inside an industrial steel shed. In Maastrict, the Netherlands, a bookstore situated inside a historic Dominican church is a pretty good approximation—to my mind—of paradise on Earth.

Artist Rachel Whiteread cast a concrete sculpture of a Victorian terraced house and placed it on an empty block that had once been lined with such homes for working-class Londoners. It served as a collective memory device, a heavy ghost of the block's built past. (Rachel Whiteread; *House*, 1993; 193 Grove Road, London E3. Destroyed 1993. © Rachel Whiteread; Photo by Sue Omerod. Courtesy the artist and Gagosian)

Photographer Richard Nickel documented metal scavengers leaving the former Chicago residence of architect–engineer Dankmar Adler, which was demolished three days later. (Dankmar Adler Residence, Adler and Sullivan, architects. Photo 1961. Richard Nickel Archive, Ryerson and Burnham Art and Architecture Archives, The Art Institute of Chicago. Digital File # 201006_110815-C61)

And yet, in disinvested communities, historic buildings—resplendent with just as many lovely, creative opportunities—are being lost, continuing the cycle of disinvestment. This chapter explores some of the reasons why, to build a foundation for understanding how community residents and professionals can find a different way forward.

Elimination: The Fallacy of a Clean Slate

When populations recede, what's left is an outsized infrastructure. Population reduction leaves a plentiful supply of buildings but no demand. Property values plummet. Access to capital and other resources dries up in inverse proportion to outward flow, like the slow and squeaky turning off of a tap.[8] The Center for Community Progress explains sustained or increasing vacancy (or "systemic vacancy") as a looped cycle. A once-vibrant neighborhood faces equity challenges (such as discriminatory or predatory lending), external triggers (such as a natural disaster or an economic crisis), a market shift (demand decreases), and then increased vacancy. The impacts of increased vacancy can fuel further challenges and perpetuate the cycle.[9]

When communities experience disinvestment, buildings can suffer what is called demolition by neglect, which is the gradual and terminal deterioration of a structure due to lack of maintenance. For example, if a roof leak is unrepaired, water eventually weakens and destroys the structure. Sometimes demolition by neglect occurs when, despite good intentions, owners lack the funds or technical resources to maintain the structure. When real estate prices bottom out, owners who do have access to funds often choose not to invest in maintaining a building because of the diminished property values and what is perceived as a negative rate of return.

When large numbers of buildings experience demolition by neglect, distress, abandonment, and vacancy, a community's aesthetic becomes a constant visual reminder of brokenness. Consequently, the vacant and distressed properties can acquire misplaced or disproportionate blame for holding back the community from progress. Overwhelming infrastructure needs, and their cascading drain on physical and emotional resources, can lead to a call for removal.

Demolition campaigns to remove the so-called blighted structures are often welcomed, even called for, by neighborhood residents. Vacant and abandoned structures pose risks to their neighbors that can harm health,

Unattended property: a frozen waterfall from a burst pipe flows out of a vacant house in Detroit that was in otherwise good condition, 2006. (Amy Hetletvedt)

Is demolition the best solution? An exalted excavator above an open field in rural Michigan, 2024. (Amy Hetletvedt)

emotional wellbeing, and municipal revenue.[10] These effects can compound conditions in the neighborhood and perpetuate the cycle of vacancy. Overwhelmed by the magnitude of vacant, abandoned, and distressed structures, residents may see demolition as the best option.

In Detroit, a Blight Removal Task Force was convened in 2014 to assess the city's building stock. The task force identified over 40,000 blighted structures, plus 38,000 structures with strong indicators to become blighted. In total, 78,000 structures or nearly 30 percent of all existing structures in the city were identified as blighted and needing intervention.[11] More than 15,000 homes were eventually demolished, with the final house under the federal demolition funds coming down in August 2020.[12] "The pace of the demolition program," according to a publication by think tank Detroit Future City, "earned the City the recognition of running the largest demolition program in the country."[13]

In the years after the work of the Blight Removal Task Force in Detroit, a majority of Detroiters held favorable views on the city's blight elimination efforts.[14] Many of the problem properties were gone. Indeed, many community safety problems—such as the potential for an unsecured cornice to fall on a pedestrian or the potential for an abandoned building to harbor criminal activity—disappear with the demolition of the distressed buildings.

Yet where the built and natural environments are concerned, a clean slate is a fallacy. Building materials and demolition debris go somewhere, usually to a landfill.[15] The presence of distressed and abandoned structures has been linked to public health problems,[16] but so have their demolition and removal. One study associated demolitions with elevated blood lead levels in Detroit children from 2014 to 2017.[17] Studies are ongoing.

In view of community and public health issues related to the built environment, it is interesting that the word *blight*—often used for communities with high rates of vacancy and abandonment—originates from a term for a diseased plant. The Center for Community Progress explains, "Consider the etymology of blight and where it places the blame. The term blight was first used in the sixteenth century to describe botanical disease that led to spreading lesions that decimated crops—something seen as an act of nature, difficult to predict or prevent. So, when applied to properties, the subtext is clear: Blight is random and blameless. But the systemic vacancy that leads to abandoned and deteriorated buildings is anything but random. It is the consequence of a legacy of intentional disinvestment, poverty, unjust policies, and racist systems."[18]

But if disinvestment is a cause of blight, is demolition really its cure? Or is it a permanent solution to something that could have been addressed differently—like an unnecessary or premature amputation?

Not all buildings can be saved, and communities do need to change over time. But our society demonstrates, at many levels, a knee-jerk tendency to erase and delete rather than to edit. Indiscriminate, hasty, or broad-scale demolition permanently removes resources that have potential benefit.[19]

Exploitation and Exportation

In the late eighteenth century, the aesthetic ideal of the Picturesque—that historical artifacts are endowed with an unintentional and inherent beauty—gained momentum through the writings of William Gilpin, Edmund Burke, Denis Diderot, and others. Estate gardens of wealthy landowners began to sprout follies, decayed classical buildings that were constructed in a ruinous state because the ruins were considered beautiful.

It was pure stage setting, an emphasis on experience designed to provoke an emotional reaction to perceived sublimity. Decay became a foil for the abundance of the wealthy and the sense of control enabled by their wealth. It was a fetish of the "haves." And so it's worth considering that the perception of beauty in decay depends heavily on one's vantage point and that economic status has something to do with it.

Architect Sidney Robinson writes of the Picturesque movement, "Not having the money or the time to correct the depredations of gravity, water, growth and decay is one thing. To cultivate them is another." He concludes this exploration by noting, "The ideals of novelty, surprise, and relaxation depend on intermittency. Repetition renders them dull and inert."[20] In other words, decay can be picturesque if it is a condition from which one has an escape.

This dichotomy in the perception of ruins isn't just a relic of yesteryear. In 2016, artist Ryan Mendoza partially deconstructed a house in Detroit and exported it to an art exhibit in Rotterdam and later to a permanent collection in Antwerp. Removing portions of the structure, which he called "The White House," left behind the gaping skeletal remains of the donor house on Detroit's West Side.

The late-seventeenth- and early-eighteenth-century upper class exhibited a fascination with elaborate miniatures and curiosity cabinets. (The doll house of Petronella Oortman, anonymous, c. 1686–c. 1710. Public domain. In the collection of the Rijksmuseum, Amsterdam, https://id.rijksmuseum.nl/2002678)

Although Mendoza discussed it as a form of connection,[21] others perceived it differently. "I feel disrespected to the max," said neighbor Beverly Wuong in a *Detroit Free Press* interview.[22]

This outrage and sense of disrespect is like that fueled by ruins porn, a term that denotes the photographic exploitation of ruinous structures. Architecture writer and critic Catherine Slessor explains that ruins porn "shamefully overlooks and overwrites the voices of those who still call the city home. Through its reductivist and disassociative prism, endemic social injustices such as poverty, marginalization and racism are ignored or ridiculed."[23]

Brian Farkas, a Detroit Building Authority project manager, said of Mendoza's White House project, "You can't do this in Detroit anymore. This is not everyone's canvas. These are neighborhoods. People live here."[24] In later chapters, I explore the idea of neighborhood as canvas and the ways in which large-scale artistic endeavors can have potential benefit.

A more recent dollhouse. Here, Shonibare's dollhouse recreates a Victorian terraced house in miniature, covering some of the furniture with traditional Nigerian fabric. The reduced scale and depiction of house as plaything call the viewer's attention to the tendency to objectify others. (Yinka Shonibare, Untitled [Dollhouse]; from the 2002 Peter Norton Family Christmas Project, resin, plastic, wood, paper, and fabric. 33.02 × 20 × 26.04 cm. © Yinka Shonibare CBE. All Rights Reserved, DACS/ ARS, NY 2024. University of Michigan Museum of Art, The Dorothy and Herbert Vogel Collection: Fifty Works for Fifty States, a joint initiative of the Trustees of the Dorothy and Herbert Vogel Collection and the National Gallery of Art, with generous support from the National Endowment for the Arts and the Institute for Museum and Library Services, 2008/2.256)

Exportation and exploitation of vacant buildings, though quantitatively much smaller in scope than removal by demolition, have an outsize psychological impact on community residents. Exportation and removal are rife with ethical questions about intent, belonging, and protection. Drew Philp, author (and owner) of *A $500 House in Detroit*, recounts a conversation with his friend Nate about whether he should salvage the front door from the abandoned house across the street for use in his own house.

> "Ahh, it's fine. It's going to go to waste if you don't. They're going to tear that house down. Or it'll be taken by someone else. You're really protecting it," Nate said earnestly. His argument seemed like the same one used to take mummies from the pyramids and justify them sitting

> in the British Museum alongside other antiquities removed for "protection" during colonialism. But this wasn't Egypt, this was Detroit and this wasn't a pyramid, it was an abandoned house. What I was going to do would technically be stealing, but from whom? A memory? The people who had abandoned it? The governments that allowed it to fester? . . . I looked around and it didn't seem as though anyone was on the street, so Nate and I headed over and ripped the door from its hinges.[25]

Philp's conversation with his friend touched on many of the contextual issues of material loss. In a sculpture called *Urban Extract* in the collection of the Detroit Institute of Arts, artist Charles McGee presents a building extract as object. The extract includes the window of a barber shop that McGee frequented for many years.[26] The piece is a poignant exploration of the severing effects of demolition and extraction on memory and cultural connections.

The magnitude of disinvestment in communities such as Detroit has caused many to view demolition as the best solution to a burdensome problem or to view so-called blighted communities as a source for further exploitation and extraction. Yet in both cases, removing resources from a community removes potential opportunities to use those resources in creative remaking. What is being lost is not only the buildings themselves but their potential benefit as physical and sociological materials for rebuilding.

Barriers in Historic Preservation Standards and Designation

Although access to capital is an obvious reason that buildings are not rehabilitated in disinvested communities, it is not the only reason. It's important to consider the barriers that current systems within the built environment may present. Some of these barriers are in the operational norms of the architecture and preservation professions.

In a 2019 article titled "Why Historic Preservation Needs a New Approach," Patrice Frey, former president of Main Street America, outlines several challenges to the field of historic preservation, among them the languishing and loss of historic buildings in disinvested real estate markets. "Valuable historic resources lie fallow because demand for space is low and the economics of rehabilitation can be extraordinarily challenging," she says.[27]

Frey doesn't blame the absence of investment alone for the loss of buildings in disinvested communities. She turns to preservation standards and strategies. "Our toolbox," says Frey, "has not evolved to keep pace. . . . Our core preservation tools do not serve all kinds of preservation well."

"Our toolbox has not evolved to keep pace."
—Patrice Frey

Frey takes as an example a two-story brick commercial building in an economically struggling small town. Although it is not especially significant as an architectural resource, it is uniquely significant to the community as an eatery and social hub. "To rehab it in a historically 'correct' way—that is, through the stringent application [of] the Standards for Rehabilitation—would be extraordinarily challenging in a town where building valuations are low, traditional financing options are scarce, and historic preservation tax credits are not a likely source of financing."[28]

The standards for preservation projects in the United States have evolved little from those established and codified in the 1960s and 1970s. The US Secretary of the Interior's Standards for the Treatment of Historic Properties offer four categories of treatment: preservation, rehabilitation, restoration, and reconstruction. These categories are organized by their level of intervention in the historic property. Preservation is the least invasive; reconstruction is the most invasive.

Within the discipline of historic preservation, the question about how much to intervene in a building—and thus the idea of organizing the standards according to level of intervention—goes back to debates rooted in the nineteenth century.

Frenchman Eugène Emmanuel Viollet-le-Duc was the architect for the restoration of Notre Dame in Paris in the mid-1800s. The building wasn't in great shape at that time, having suffered decline and significant damage during the French Revolution. Viollet-le-Duc designed the spire with which we are now familiar at Notre Dame, the spire that burned in the April 2019 fire. (After much debate, the spire has been reconstructed to Viollet-le-Duc's version.[29])

The spire wasn't historically authentic to the Gothic cathedral. It was Viollet-le-Duc's historicist vision of the spire, the spire he believed should have been there. Viollet-le-Duc viewed restoration as returning the building to a complete state that had perhaps never existed at any particular moment in the past.[30]

In contrast to Viollet-le-Duc's passion for revisionist restoration, Englishman John Ruskin, his contemporary, "abhorred restoration of any kind and defended the aesthetic value of ruins."[31] Rather than engage in speculative or even historically defensible restoration, Ruskin emphasized the moral and memorial role of the structures of the past and said, “We have no right to touch them. They are not ours.”[32]

Viollet-le-Duc’s approach to intervention was very heavy, Ruskin’s was very light. Over time, the lighter approach won over, and later voices in the nineteenth and early twentieth centuries, such as that of William Morris, argued for the value of leaving changes that had taken place over time.

The interesting dilemma for disinvested communities today is that although older buildings that are considered nonhistoric are opportunities for more experimental and less financially burdensome approaches, designation can give them a helpful visibility to attract funding. Yet, the nature of the designation process and the need to establish of a period of significance reveal a disproportionate focus on conserving buildings as a monument to a particular period of history or as a historic artifact (a precious object) rather than on the role of the building to serve a community’s needs or its potential for storytelling.[33]

Buildings in disinvested communities may have lost character-defining features of their architecture to vandalism or decay or may have been substantially adapted for different uses over the years. Referring to the criteria for listing on the National Register of Historic Places, former president of the National Trust for Historic Preservation Stephanie Meeks says, “Those are very high standards to meet, and although standards are important, this high bar tends to limit our perspective of history to architectural significance. There is so much more to our story than that.”[34] When character-defining features are foregrounded, what other features (physical, cultural, social) recede to the background?[35]

The good news is that work is being done to refine the municipal and regulatory systems for buildings (historic and other) and to consider how these systems could be adapted in the context of disinvested communities. Flexible and multilayered approaches are needed to support revitalization efforts in disinvested communities.[36]

In 2023, the National Conference of State Historic Preservation Officers (NCSHPO) committee released a report on the National Register for Historic Places that advocated, among other recommendations, to “consider adding new criterion for recognition of places of cultural significance that may not retain integrity as traditionally understood, but that may hold deep importance and meaning to groups and communities.”[37]

In March 2023, the NCSHPO formed a working group to provide recommendations on the standards and their application. American Institute of Architects Historic Resources Committee chair Robert Burns commented, "Our understanding of the need for historic preservation to take on a more holistic view of sustainability including social, cultural, and economic equality . . . calls for us to look closely as to whether current standards are inclusive or exclusive."[38]

Historic preservation professionals, architects, and students of those disciplines must contribute to shaping policy, participation models, codes, and standards so that they function better in all communities. In the context of disinvested communities, open dialogues, more flexible standards, and expanded definitions will respect the changes that have taken place over time and encourage preserving with purposes that align with broader use, narrative, or developmental goals in a community.

Barriers in Process: Financing and Delivering Professional Services

A finished product, where buildings and especially houses are concerned, is very much a construct of the so-called first world. If you've lived or traveled elsewhere, no doubt you're familiar with the sight of rebar (steel reinforcing bars) sticking up from the second story of a masonry house. In much of the world, many houses are self-built, but even when they're not, building one's house is much more of an incremental process. Rooms are added, floors are added.

One reason for this is financing. The mortgage industry in the United States focuses on the all-at-once. If a homeowner seeks a construction or renovation finance loan, there's a limited period within which the work must be completed so that the mortgage company has turnkey collateral for the loan. But in parts of the world where housing loans are uncommon or unattainable, construction is self-financed. And self-financing is not done all at once.

Modern architecture and preservation project delivery is based on a triangular structure of participants: the professional (an architect, conservator, or historic preservation specialist), the client (individual, corporation, or nonprofit), and the municipal authorities (the entities that regulate the project and its development). The client initiates the process because the client brings the funding for the project, whether cash, mortgage, grants, or other financing schemes such as tax credits. The proposed end use for the building shapes the extent of the renovation or rehabilitation project.

The trigger for the cycle and the actualization of a project is funding, and the operation is transactional. The project moves around the triangle in a series of personal, financial, and regulatory transactions. This basic operating structure has been in place since the development of modern building codes and the professionalization of architecture and preservation in the nineteenth and twentieth centuries. Although these project delivery norms work well in many contexts, they do not necessarily function well in disinvested communities.

Low property values that result from disinvestment are obstacles for reinvestment, and there is little space to denominate other types of resources. This challenge is an opening to explore and expand ways that clients and communities can work with professionals to acknowledge the expertise and agency of both parties, in smaller increments that require less capital and are more adaptable. Some ingredients for this co-participation are discussed in Chapter 3.

Disinvested communities don't have the same level of access to financial and technical resources as other communities. Often, multiple systems—including physical infrastructure systems and sociopolitical systems—are broken or functioning suboptimally, and the standards and delivery models for interventions in historic buildings do not always work well. But waiting for the fix often leads to more loss.

I do not believe that widespread demolition is the answer for approaching vacant, abandoned, and distressed buildings in disinvested communities. So far, there's not a lot of evidence that the immense postrecession demolition efforts have benefited Detroit. Time will tell. But I wonder, along the parallel timeline of a path not taken, what creativity and the Detroit community could have wrought with the raw materials of their history.

Preserving with Purpose explores contextual approaches to existing buildings in disinvested communities as an alternative to demolition, explains why these buildings matter, and what communities and professionals can make of them, together.

Detail from Candy Chang's public installation "I wish this was." Ongoing from 2012. (Candy Chang)

Chapter 2

Why Buildings Matter: Purposes for Preserving

"The tragedy is not that things are broken.

The tragedy is that they are not mended again."

—Alan Paton, *Cry, the Beloved Country*

When vacant, abandoned, and distressed buildings are eliminated, the problems that they represent may disappear, but so does their potential. It's a loss that can't be retrieved.

Sociologist Eric Klinenberg's early work was rooted in questions he asked about the physical structure of communities and health outcomes in Chicago following the heat wave of 1995.[1] In his latest book, *Palaces for the People: How Social Infrastructure Can Help Fight Inequality, Polarization, and the Decline of Civic Life*, he defines social infrastructure as "the physical places and organizations that shape the way people interact." He clarifies that "social infrastructure is not 'social capital'—a concept commonly used to measure people's relationships and interpersonal networks—but the physical conditions that determine whether social capital develops."[2]

Klinenberg's studies in Chicago demonstrated that where other factors—such as poverty and racial demographics—were the same, South Side

Chicago neighborhoods with less abandonment had better public health outcomes during exceptional events. "In places like Englewood, the shoddy social infrastructure discouraged interaction and impeded mutual support, whereas in places like Auburn Gresham the social infrastructure encouraged those things," he noted.[3]

Thriving communities with robust social infrastructure have buildings. When decay and demolition hollow out a community, poorer social infrastructure can negatively affect residents. In disinvested communities, particularly, retaining and rehabilitating existing buildings is critical. Although retaining buildings means that the potential for gentrification is greater, extensive demolition decreases the likelihood of socioeconomic recovery. Says planner Alan Mallach, "Gentrifying areas are rarely the most distressed areas of a city, particularly those where the cumulative effect of demolishing vacant buildings has undone the neighborhood's fabric. . . . Indeed, the idea one hears that urban demolition is a stalking horse for future gentrification is yet another urban myth; in reality, it more often creates a moonscape of vacant land that all but guarantees gentrification will *not* take place."[4]

Existing buildings matter to social infrastructure, to economic regeneration, and to healthy communities. Though distressed or abandoned, existing buildings have embedded possibilities and energies that can benefit their communities and can tell stories that are important to healing us all.

Environmental Benefits, Embedded Possibilities

Abandoned or distressed buildings are often seen as an environmental burden. Indeed, existing buildings often contain environmental hazards such as lead and asbestos that must be properly remediated. But eliminating existing buildings does not obviate remediation because even demolition requires environmental remediation.

Some characterize architectural salvage as the environmental and economic upside to demolition. When buildings are deconstructed and materials are salvaged, they can be reused and add value to artisanal products or other building rehabilitations. Yet, as discussed in Chapter 1, salvage operations can also be a way to extract from a disinvested community, and although deconstruction can be an environmentally kinder alternative to demolition, it still precludes later possibilities for the use and value of the structure.

From an environmental perspective, it is almost always more sustainable to reuse an existing building than to build new because the construction process is so resource intensive.[5] Based on an analysis of a damaged multifamily building in Spain, a study in the *Environmental Impact Assessment Review* concludes that "even with a severely damaged building, the repair and retrofit work incurs a lower economic and environmental impact than that of a total replacement with a new construction."[6]

The concept of *embodied energy* refers to the total energy consumption over a building's lifespan, from the raw and extractive energy of the building materials, to the energy consumed in the construction process and the energy used in maintaining the building. In an article called "Embodied Energy and Historic Preservation," Mike Jackson calculates that even if salvage practices are used in demolition and the new building constructed in place of the demolished building is energy-efficient, it would take fifty-seven years before a net energy savings is achieved.[7]

As architecture critic Thomas De Monchaux says, "So much of a building's lifetime ecological and energetic impact comes through the operations of initial material extraction, manufacturing, transportation, and construction; and then of eventual demolition, further transportation, and decay. Sustainable buildings are therefore not new buildings—however fuel-efficient their machines and materials. Sustainable buildings are buildings that have been sustained."[8]

"Sustainable buildings are buildings that have been sustained."
—Thomas De Monchaux

Residents in a disinvested community may ask, "Why should we lead the way?" If the environmental benefit of keeping and reusing buildings is good for the whole planet, why should a disinvested community bear the burden of rehabilitating the building? One answer comes from reframing the perspective. De Monchaux defined sustainable buildings as buildings *that have been sustained*. But buildings also have the capacity *to sustain*. A building can be approached as a resource to the community.

Opening up possibilities for an existing building *to sustain*, to lend its resources while it's waiting for its next act, can recapture or capitalize on the embodied energy of the building. This is true not only in terms of the fossil fuels and material values that the building represents but also in terms of its embedded social value. Existing buildings contain possibilities to benefit disinvested communities—some in ways that are very practical and others in ways that lean more toward the poetic or narrative.

This building-as-gas-can graphic connected the growing historic preservation movement with the energy conservation and environmental movement, 1980. (© National Trust for Historic Preservation, available through the Missouri Historical Society, St. Louis)

Practical Benefits: The Prosaic

"Twenty-Four Reasons Historic Preservation Is Good for Your Community," a 2020 publication by Place Economics, summarizes numerous studies on the economic benefits of heritage preservation.[9] Some of these benefits, such as increased property values, are not as relevant to disinvested communities, where property values may continue to remain low in a cycle of systemic vacancy, but others—such as business incubation and tourism—can reintroduce use into vacant buildings and have positive impacts in a disinvested community.

Use value is one of a spectrum of values that has been recognized in the development of historic preservation as a discipline. As categorized by Alois Riegl, early-twentieth-century art historian, these values are intentional monuments (made to commemorate something), historical monuments (sites that become significant over time), and age-value monuments. Riegl also recognized what he called noncommemorative values for the present day, which include use value, newness value, and relative art value.[10] All of the values have a place within historic preservation projects around the world. But in the context of disinvested communities, use value (or what I call in this book *prosaic*, *practical value* or *practical benefits*) plays a particularly important role.

"It's not about the building itself for communities or how the building looks, it's the use that it serves," says Claudia Guerra, a San Antonio, Texas (US) cultural historian.[11] Guerra points out that although use value is acknowledged in preservation theory, it is not often a part of the preservation review process in a municipality because use is usually regulated by zoning. Use value, the way in which a building or space fills a social need, gives a structure purpose.

Preservation advocate Rosanne Haggerty has said that preservation "carries a key lesson for those concerned with rising inequality in our cities: all buildings and designed spaces were initially built to solve problems, and many were built to solve social problems."[12] A potential new use may or may not be related to a building's original use, but it can answer some social need. Could it be shelter for someone who needs it or a workshop for a new business venture? Could it be a container for a cultural archive? Could it be a living school for needed skills—a training academy of sorts? Could it be a place to grow food?

Artist Candy Chang's public installation "I wish this was," invites residents to engage in dialogue with each other and with vacant buildings in their community by recording their thoughts on name tags attached to the structures. (A photo from this exhibit appears on page 26). This inclusive approach encourages in situ thinking that, as Chang says, "reframe[s] empty buildings in terms of their potential identities."[13] Passersby can record their thoughts about how an underused building could meet a need, and the name-tag stickers become a kind of public discussion.

The Bánffy Castle in Romania (profiled in Chapter 6) needed numerous repairs, but its large and varied spaces also offered the opportunity for professionals and craftspeople to learn and practice the skills of historic preservation. It now hosts the Built Heritage Conservation training program, where under the guidance of knowledgeable professionals, participants can gain a variety of skills in heritage conservation. By serving as a resource for education in the preservation trades, the Bánffy Castle is slowly being restored.

In a small Italian village north of Naples facing extensive depopulation, the group behind the Million Donkey Hotel project (profiled in Chapter 6) saw an opportunity to increase economic activity while benefiting the community and tourists: The empty, abandoned spaces in the community could cater to the desire of the modern traveler for an inexpensive and authentic accommodation experience. The rustic, lightly furnished, networked hotel rooms created in empty spaces around the village benefited travelers and the community through affordable tourism and shared experiences.

Narrative Benefits: The Poetic

Historical monuments is one of the three primary categories in Reigl's historic preservation classification. Historical monuments are structures that were not constructed as monuments but tell a story that a society later wants to remember. In a disinvested community, these stories and narratives can be lost when buildings are lost, resulting in a social amnesia of certain important histories, whether hopeful or distressing.

The loss of these stories affects the way that history is read or remembered through our built environment, rendering silent the communities—often with significant minority populations—whose artifacts are gone.

According to the Center for American Progress, only 24 percent of US national parks and monuments recognize diverse peoples and cultures.[14] On a global scale, as of 2023, nearly 50 percent of UNESCO world heritage sites are in Europe or North America, and less than 10 percent are in Africa.[15] The buildings and narratives of Western civilization still dominate these recognized heritage sites.

Each year, the National Trust for Historic Preservation publishes its "11 Most Endangered Properties" list to raise awareness of designated and yet-to-be designated properties and structures that are at risk for demolition or loss. The National Trust does not provide analysis about the properties on this list, but in my informal assessment of their descriptions of the endangerment, about a third of these properties in any given year can be said to be at risk due to disinvestment, the lack of funds, or the lack of a client (with funds).

The World Monuments Watch cites four global challenges to significant heritage sites: climate change, underrepresentation, imbalanced tourism, and crisis recovery.[16] Regarding underrepresentation, the Watch states, "Greater efforts should be made to amplify narratives that tell a more textured, just and complete story of humanity."[17] Whether overlooked or imperiled, in the United States and around the world, stories are going untold.

The way that buildings can articulate and amplify stories is what I call *poetic, narrative value* or *narrative benefits*. Buildings tell stories about technology, tools, material, and climate through their construction. Their form, ornamentation, and organization tell stories about cultural values—who belonged, who didn't belong, which activities were celebrated, which activities were hidden. Like elders and epics, they also tell us stories about the things they've seen.

Historically, surveyors have used witness trees to mark boundary lines of property. A witness tree is located near or at the corner of a property boundary and is traditionally marked by three parallel axe hacks. According to an American Forest Management article, "Surveyors use hacks or chop marks in the tree because when the tree heals a scar will remain. This scar can remain visible for decades as evidence to the location of the boundary line."[18]

Buildings also serve as witnesses to history. And sometimes, like witness trees, buildings bear scars. This was the case with both the Cathedral Church of St. Michael in Coventry and St. Luke's in Liverpool, UK (both discussed in Chapter 5). The communities of these churches, which were bombed in World War II, chose to leave the buildings as a partial ruin in memory of the war and the lives lost. Ben Roy's Service Station in the southern United States, also profiled in Chapter 5, can serve as a viewpoint to the tragic events that proceeded from an encounter at the adjacent Bryant Grocery, now in a state of ruin.

A distressed environment can be the subject of harmful one-sided narratives. A report from the Power of the Commons initiative, a demonstration about the power of public spaces, explains, "In addition to challenges tied directly to disinvestment, these neighborhoods, many of them majority Black, are also the subject of harmful media narratives that focus on negative statistics such as crime and unemployment rather than the culture, creativity or historical significance of the community. This one-sided storytelling creates stigma, fear and a sense among outsiders that a neighborhood is a place to avoid."[19] The report cites studies in Chicago by sociologist Robert Sampson showing that a neighborhood's reputation was a greater predictor of poverty five years later than even the existing poverty level.[20] The narratives told about a place have a powerful effect on shaping the place.

The Kauffman Foundation has noted that the persistent narrative that rural communities are somewhere to escape from misses the "critical political, demographic, and economic nuances that reveal a more complicated story—as well as the compelling pull of rural spaces in a post-pandemic America. . . . Viewing rural spaces as an American relic of a disappearing world ignores the innovative spirit that made these diverse communities vibrant in the first place. That innovation and diversity remains key to the future of rural communities."[21]

Multilayered stories are needed, not only for memorializing their past but as a powerful, effective force in shaping the future of disinvested communities. Retaining and telling the stories of the built environment in disinvested communities tilts the balance toward a more just and equitable society by presenting a fuller picture of the cultural heritage of the region or nation.

In our fractured sociocultural landscape, the physical resources that tell the stories of minority populations can foster empathy and understanding from those outside those populations. Historian and author Dolores Hayden reflects on philosopher Edward S. Casey's idea of place memory. "Place memory," she says, "encapsulates the human ability to connect with both the built and natural environments that are entwined in the cultural landscape. It is the key to the power of historic places to help citizens define the public pasts: places trigger memories for insiders, who have shared a common past, and at the same time places often can represent shared pasts to outsiders who might be interested in knowing about them in the present."[22]

The International Coalition of Sites of Conscience notes that at traumatic or difficult sites, "the need to remember often competes with the equally strong pressure to forget. Even with the best of intentions—such as to promote reconciliation after trauma by 'turning the page'—erasing the past can prevent new generations from learning critical lessons and destroy opportunities to establish peace now and well into the future."[23]

Many members of the Sites of Conscience network function as museums. But it's not only museums that can foster empathy and understanding. Temporarily functioning buildings and structures in various stages of repair and renewal (such as those profiled in Chapter 6), building- and neighborhood-scaled art sculptures, and sites of remembrance (such as those in Chapter 5) can benefit disinvested communities in both practical and poetic ways and help to build a more civil, compassionate society.

In a short film about the Menokin project, which is profiled in Chapter 8, Tom Duckenfield, a descendant of the enslaved laborers at the Menokin plantation, said, "Because of its varied history, Menokin can serve as a place of convening. And in convening, we can learn how to understand each other more. We can heal the scars from the past."[24]

Power of Persistence: Priorities

Persistence—not in the sense of trying again but in the sense of persisting, remaining—can be a powerful statement in the context of a disinvested community. Sometimes just remaining standing can be an act of resistance. Edith Macefield famously resisted selling her home and land to a developer in the Ballard neighborhood of Seattle in the early 2000s. The image of her home surrounded by an apartment building symbolizes her resistance to development pressure. An act of resistance to demolition or decay can be just as powerful. Staying is an act of resistance against the forces of destruction, be they neglect, nature, or human-initiated negation.

The approach that I call *priority* does not offer an immediate practical use or interpretive experience for the community like the *prosaic (practical)* and *poetic (narrative)* approaches discussed above. Rather, it is about simply keeping a building, or portion of a building or site, that the community has identified as important. It is about choosing continuance.

When an individual or community chooses to prioritize a building and to take some action to ensure its continuity, that resistance is a declaration.

Although the purpose of the priority approach is less tangible than the practical or even the poetic, it has great power. The force of resistance, in terms of physics, must be equal to or greater than the force that it's resisting. So resistance—persistence, continuation—is an act of power and an act of intentional curation.

In a community facing systemic vacancy, there are more buildings that could potentially be saved than there are economic resources to save them. There are also more buildings that could potentially be saved than there are personal or collective energies to save them. Some worthy buildings may or must be left behind. Therefore, it is important for a community to inventory their built infrastructure, identifying significant sites, stories, and other cultural resources and—regarding the buildings—evaluate the level of risk, deterioration, and ease of intervention.

A historic photograph of Edith Macefield sits on the kitchen counter of her Seattle home, 2008. (Stuart Isett/www.isett.com)

Neighborhood Inventory: Buildings and Values

Action (or inaction) in the built environment, by default, expresses priorities and power dynamics. When communities come together to set priorities and articulate purposes for preserving buildings in their built environment, they can beneficially shape what lies ahead.

This section discusses some ways that community residents—on their own or alongside an architect or preservationist—can inventory buildings and identify values in their communities. In the early 2000s, for example, an initiative called Invisible Zagreb began populating a database of abandoned properties in the city. Later, temporary events and test uses of interventions in the spaces contributed to a collective reimagining between citizens and the municipality.[25]

Edith Macefield's house surrounded by development in the Ballard neighborhood of Seattle, 2008. (Stuart Isett/www.isett.com)

Ownership is a primary factor in evaluating the ease of potential intervention in a building. Tax records are a good place to start. If a property is on a foreclosure, tax delinquency, or demolition list, it is likely to be at risk of being lost and could be a priority for intervention. (If there are land banks in the community, check to see which properties are in ownership of the land bank.) The quality, condition, and immediate context of the building are also important factors.

In his article "A Preservation Movement for All Americans," David Brown, former chief preservation officer at the National Trust for Historic Preservation, suggests that citizens take advantage of geographic information systems and open data systems to undertake their own mapping of community buildings.[26] Citing architectural historian James Marston Fitch's assertion[27] that citizen participation is critical to the future of preservation, Brown ties citizen participation with emerging technologies and means of mapping space. There are numerous detailed resources about how communities can inventory their building stock.[28] Once identified, communities have historically used visual markers, both formal and informal, to declare buildings of value.

Recording stories is a vital element of the inventory process. Collecting narratives—especially the narratives of minority groups that have historically been excluded or overlooked—is at the core of one of the three approaches discussed in this chapter. Gathering these stories is at least as important as gathering other data about buildings, such as condition and ownership. There are many creative ways to elicit and compile narratives—for example, training and deploying teens to interview community elders to start community story banks.

The US city of San Antonio, Texas, has experimented with various strategies for designation surveys. *Plática*, Spanish for *conversation* or *chat*, is the term used for the city's process to discuss proposed changes and elicit stories from community members.[29] As Claudia Guerra, cultural historian in San Antonio's Office of Historic Preservation, explains, "We do a lot of oral history. We ask people to map out the places that are important to them. We might do a windshield survey because we need to get a sense of the neighborhood, but we look at it through their eyes first."[30]

Although the *pláticas* to which Guerra refers were undertaken by the municipality, residents can initiate these conversations themselves to determine which buildings and stories they find to be important. In addition to residents and municipalities identifying buildings and stories that are important to preserve, communities can also identify values that will guide their efforts. Sometimes this needs to happen in a very deliberate way. For example, if mitigating displacement or creating pathways for long-term residents to remain in the neighborhood is a value, communities can look to organizational models and ownership vehicles such as community land trusts or community benefit agreements. For example, the Granby Four Streets neighborhood in Liverpool, discussed in Chapter 9, valued maintaining affordability throughout their revitalization efforts, so they implemented a community land trust and sale pricing restrictions on properties that they owned.

In Berlin, Germany, the team behind the project ExRotaprint, in the complex of a former printing press manufacturer, established a legal framework that set up the building under a ninety-nine-year heritable building right and nonprofit ownership. The spaces are affordably leased for a mix of work, arts, and community activities that benefit the immediate neighborhood. According to ExRotaprint, the intentional model and legal structure mean that "the complex has been withdrawn from property speculation for the long-term. . . . The profit of the project lies in the stability it offers and the ways it is used—today and in the future."[31]

Sometimes a value that guides an individual or a series of projects emerges in a more organic way, based on intergenerational relationships and conversation. Resident activists and artists often describe an "a-ha" moment that clarified their values and shaped projects that changed their communities. Rick Lowe, founder of Project Row Houses, describes in Chapter 10 how a question from a high school student moved him out of the studio and into the neighborhood. Tyree Guyton, creator of the Heidelberg Project in Detroit, which is profiled in Chapter 5, explained his "a-ha" moment this way: "I knew that I was on to something the very first minute I went out there to make a polka dot."[32]

A 2024 show at the Contemporary Arts Museum Houston included a photo series about the Brick Street Protest, which occurred in 2015 in Freedmen's Town in Houston's Fourth Ward. The protest ignited when residents saw city workers removing historic bricks from the streets of the community, which was the first settlement for freed Black residents in Houston after the Civil War. One of the exhibit curators, Charonda Johnson, was out on a walk that day and remembered her mentor Lue Williams's words: "If you see people coming to get these bricks, that's a red alert emergency."[33] A temporary restraining order stopped the work, and the bricks that had been removed were replaced in 2018.[34] The Freedmen's Town Brick Street Protest is an

This blue shield on a building in Belgium identifies a cultural resource protected under the Hague Convention for the Protection of Cultural Property in the Event of Armed Conflict (signed in 1954), 2014. (Amy Hetletvedt)

example of how community values shaped and coalesced a *priority* response to retain a community resource.

German artist Joseph Beuys (1921–1986) is credited with coining the term *social sculpture* to define his work. Beuys infused his ideas about society into his artistic practice, inviting others into collective action. These collective actions, for Beuys, rested on the premise of art and creativity as capital. Dr. Martin Luther King, Jr., later expressed a similar idea in his book *Where Do We Go from Here: Chaos or Community?*, in which he states, "For the evils

of racism, poverty and militarism to die, a new set of values must be born. Our economy must become more person-centered than property- and profit-centered."[35]

A community enters or continues in a cycle of systemic vacancy when there is too much supply (of available buildings) and not enough demand (for the available buildings). Demand is created by a perception of value. And perceptions of value can be a two-edged sword.

When cultural value (built up by collective creative, sustained artistic action in the community and specifically in the built environment) gains momentum and becomes visible to those outside the community, it can begin to raise property values. The increased cultural value puts a frame around the buildings or neighborhood that becomes commodified and encoded in the prices of the buildings and rents. As will be described in the profiles in Part

This "Right to Remain" mural on a building in the warehouse district of Phoenix, Arizona, references a campaign to save buildings in the neighborhood in the face of redevelopment, 2019. (Library of Congress, Prints & Photographs Division, photo by Carol M. Highsmith [LC-DIG-highsm-55684])

III, some communities have centered their values on questioning preconceptions of value itself—of full and empty, of scarcity and abundance.

In the many ways described in this book—from the practical to the poetic—communities can approach existing buildings in purposeful ways that benefit the community as they build on resources that are inherent to the community. After all, some valuable things one can inherit, borrow, steal, or reap from the labor and legacies of others. Other valuable things one cannot.

The bottom line is that saving buildings in disinvested communities is about so much more than the physicality of the structures or their monetized value. As Andrew Hurley underscored in his essay about preservation in struggling communities, "For all of the damage inflicted by serrated

A weathered sign promising loans in "1 min[ute]" in Detroit, Michigan, 2019. (Library of Congress, Prints & Photographs Division, photo by Carol M. Highsmith [LC-DIG-highsm-60382])

streetscapes and crumbling buildings, what is truly at stake for people who remain in these places is the viability of communities as they come under assault from the pressures of population loss, infrastructure collapse, and the breakdown of social supports."[36]

Saving buildings matters. Historic and existing buildings offer economic and social opportunities for a disinvested community. They represent an environmental investment to which all of society has contributed. Buildings have a unique ability to tell a story and a role in fostering empathy through our ability to enter, experience, and be immersed in them. For these reasons, they're not only critical to the communities of which they are a part, they're critical to fostering a more compassionate, sustainable, and healthier society.

Zenna Todd's hand over an embroidered hand on a crazy quilt, 1978. (Photo by Geraldine Niva Johnson for the Blue Ridge Parkway Folklife Project. Blue Ridge Parkway Folklife Project collection [AFC 1982/009], American Folklife Center, Library of Congress. [BR8-45-20544/20])

Chapter 3

What Works: Processes and Perspectives

"The lack of resources is no longer an excuse not to act."

—Jaime Lerner, urbanist and former mayor of Curitiba, Brazil

The conversation about why so many buildings are lost in disinvested communities often begins and ends with lack: the lack of financial resources to rehabilitate them. When the perspective broadens to consider creative, material, and artistic resources that exist within and around a community and how buildings can serve a purpose for the community, the conversation can move from stalemate to starting point.

This chapter's lead image, from the Blue Ridge Parkway Folklife Project collection, shows Zenna Todd's hand over the crazy quilt she made in the late 1970s. Crazy quilts were created over years or even generations from scraps of items that were worn out, many of them precious fabrics such as velvet or silk. Crazy quilts do not follow a master pattern, make use of irregularities, and are adorned with the whimsy of fancy stitchwork and embroidery.

Like these quilts, purposeful approaches to individual buildings can form a beautiful fabric in a community over time, including a network of collaborators: residents and others who share an interest in the ideas, projects, and happenings. "I didn't have any expectations of any of it," Rick Lowe said about his and fellow artists' work in the Houston community that eventually became Project Row Houses (profiled in Chapter 10). "I was just accepting the resources of the community as they came forth . . . both internally and externally. There was the physical geographic community of people and its structures, but there was also a broader community of interest; of people who shared the ideas and desires of this project."[1]

A Perspective on Resources

This chapter discusses perspectives and identifies processes that can be helpful for reimagining buildings in disinvested communities. One of the keys to Lowe and his fellow artists' perspective was the ability to see resources rather than lack: resources that were not only inherent to the geographic community—such as its building stock and the creative and cultural resources of the residents—but of another layer of community, which could include creatives, historians, and building professionals from outside the geographic or even the cultural community.

"Repair is not a solitary act; it requires collective wisdom."
—C. L. Bohannon

Lowe continued, "I never think of the funding when starting a project. With Project Row Houses, we started with the idea that *we are* the resources to make this thing happen: our own bodies, our own creative spirits."[2]

Professor and landscape architect C. L. Bohannon, in a *Places Journal* discussion called "Field Notes on Repair," says, "Repair is not a solitary act; it requires collective wisdom." He goes on to say, "Communities can best articulate their own needs and aspirations; they can tell us about the intricate web of relationships that give purpose to their environment. In true partnership with communities, we can co-create with care, honoring the lived experiences of those who inhabit the landscapes we shape."[3]

A foundation for healthy engagement is formed when architects and other building professionals position themselves as shared generators with the community in ways that acknowledge the expertise and agency of the professional and the community members and clients. In her book *The Architectures of Spatial Justice*, architect Dana Cuff observes that "removing the primacy of owner and client—along with notions of any singular authority the architect may have held—creates a fortuitous vacancy that opens space for a critical re-reading of who inhabits the city."[4] I'd add that changing the norms or methods of practice could open space not only for who inhabits the

The Tribute Money by Masaccio (circa 1424, Brancacci Chapel, Florence, Italy) was innovative in the development of perspective (line and atmospheric). It depicts a story about finding needed resources in unexpected, nearby places—in this case, a coin in a fish. (Masaccio, Public domain, via Wikimedia Commons)

city but for who designs the city, which parts of it are saved, and its morphology over time.

One way that architects can serve as a resource is by creating an image, visualization, model, or symbol that expresses a community's values or vision for a project. This connects directly to the inventory and values process discussed in Chapter 2. Where do these sifted priorities, collected narratives, and clarified values go? Making the inventory and values accessible to the community is an important touchstone, as is keeping records and archives when possible. For example, the Sweet Water Foundation's Thought Barn on Chicago's South Side displays wood community models. The models powerfully depict how the density of the neighborhood had changed over time and are available as a reference for talking about initiatives in the neighborhood.

Guardian writer Oliver Wainwright describes how the sight of a full-size tree growing out of the living room floor of an abandoned house in the Granby Four neighborhood, which is profiled in Chapter 9, led to Assemble Studio creating "a seductive image of a tropical palm house inside the raw brick shell of the house." That image, Wainwright notes, "became a powerful symbol of new life springing from the ruins—and a useful tool to woo the Arts Council to fund the project."[5] An image that strongly reflects a community's

A community event in the Thought Barn, 2024. The models are on the white platforms at the left. (Courtesy of Sweet Water Foundation)

values or a core idea for a project is a persuasive tool to garner more resources and support.

Architects can listen and observe, and link existing community desires, initiatives, and resources to potential solutions. Assemble Studio describes how the "sustainable and incremental vision" developed for the Granby neighborhood built on what the residents had already been doing and "translates it to the refurbishment of housing, public space and the provision of new work and enterprise opportunities."[6]

Sometimes when local government is not functioning optimally, nonprofits such as community development corporations stand in the gap by creating, maintaining, and advocating for neighborhood plans. The nonprofit can be helpful to the community in the development and articulation of a vision for their spaces and in interacting with other stakeholders. There are always multiple forces at work shaping a community, and systemic decisions on transportation, water, power, and waste management at a state or federal level powerfully shape neighborhoods.

Disinvested communities are often places where the negative effects of past large-scale projects such as urban renewal or massive demolitions have been experienced most acutely. Therefore, it is vitally important for residents to understand how upcoming larger-scale plans will affect the community. At the 2024 Aspen Ideas Festival, American Civil Liberties Union president Deborah Archer discussed how visualization services added value at a juncture of critical decision making on the built environment in Indianapolis.

Initially, there was little community response when the Indiana Department of Transportation presented a proposal for a major infrastructure upgrade to the I-65/I-70 freeway junction. "They really had nothing to say," recounts Archer, "until a community member said, 'These drawings mean nothing to them and I'm going to redraw these plans in a way that shows them exactly the impact that this is going to have on their community.' And then the community was outraged, and they organized."[7] Engagement skyrocketed once this idea of translation or visualization (which eventually formed the ReThink Coalition) helped the community understand the impact of the proposal on adjacent neighborhoods and envision alternatives.

Layers of government addressing environmental problems in an Environmental Protection Administration poster from 1965. The lowest layer, in pink, addresses sanitation (waste) and abandonment. Can vacant and underused buildings be considered form of societal waste? Are they an environmental problem in the broadest sense? (Problems?: 966-: Air, water, noise, sewer. New York, Environmental Protection Administration, Sponsor/Advertiser. Yanker poster collection. Library of Congress. ([Call number POS 6-US, no. 1243. Digital id yan 1a38986])

Important considerations for any plans—whether generated very locally or from a broader government entity—are who is generating the plans, who is sanctioning the plans, and how the plans are changed and evaluated as they move forward. Urbanist Jane Jacobs, in a 1981 speech, said, "Big plans, in which everything has been foreseen as far as possible, stifle alternative possibilities and new departures."[8]

Architects, other professionals, and community development corporations can be a resource for communities as they interface with big plans, but they can also help facilitate the smaller plans that ignite alternative possibilities for disinvested communities. Working in an incremental and iterative way offers opportunity for beauty and benefit as different approaches to buildings are stitched together over time.

Incremental and Iterative Processes

Architects and other creatives, historians, and building professionals, working alongside residents and community groups in disinvested communities, can look to incremental and iterative processes as a healthy and helpful model of advancement. In the context of this discussion, *incremental* means small steps taken over time. *Iterative* means that with each break or step along the way, the results are examined to allow for adjustments as needed. The terms *incremental* and *iterative* have been linked together in the computer software industry since the 1950s.[9] Iterative and incremental software development (IID) uses repeated cycles and smaller portions to take advantage of learning in the development of large projects or to deal with changes in requirements as the project advances.

Software developers do have plans, milestones, and an end goal. But the IID process acknowledges a limited capacity to envision the end product because of what might develop or change along the way.

At the scale of a building, an incremental process can help with financing and allows greater opportunity for individuation and innovation. In disinvested communities, where low property values limit financial opportunities such as loans and mortgages, approaches to reusing or rehabilitating buildings often begin in ways that are primarily self-funded and dependent on local resources.

John F. C. Turner, a twentieth-century pioneering scholar of housing's role in development, focused on the value of incremental improvement by the owner–occupant (often called self-help housing). His work was heavily influenced by years spent living and working in Peru. Community health in the broadest sense was central to the incremental concepts that Turner described, both in the planning stages and in the outcome. "When dwellers control the major decisions and are free to make their own contributions in the design, construction, or management of their housing," Turner says, "both this process and the environment produced stimulate individual and social well-being."[10]

Of John Turner's work and philosophy, *Places Journal* critic-in-residence Cassim Shepard says, "This fundamental belief in activating the *agency* of residents—to set priorities and make decisions, and sometimes to design and build—has much to offer our present moment."[11] The incremental process enables progress on individual existing buildings, driven by the priorities and needs of the owner–occupant, despite the lack of resources for completion.

The idea of incremental self-building is conceptually and visually expressed in the firm Elemental's Villa Verde housing in Constitutión, Chile. The initial project construction, completed in 2010, offered half of a house (including the more expensive and difficult-to-construct elements such as kitchens and bathrooms and a full roof structure) to purchasers who then completed the project over time, according to their own tastes, needs, and finances.

A street of lower- and moderate-income houses built through aided and mutual self-help, administered by a government agency, in Ciudad Kennedy on the outskirts of Bogotá, Colombia. Undated photo taken five years after completion. Most of the houses built in the aided self-help program were subsequently rebuilt to higher standards by the individual households on their own unaided initiative. (Originally published in *Housing by People: Towards Autonomy in Building Environments* by John F. C. Turner, 1976. © Marion Boyars Publishers Ltd.)

Authors Clare Cumberlidge and Lucy Musgrave called Elemental's housing designs "a response to the realization that development does not consist of a finite project, but rather is an ongoing process of transformation of which physical intervention is but one part."[12] Both Turner and Elemental worked on new construction projects in areas of the world where population migration into urban areas creates a scarcity of housing. In an environment where underused buildings are plentiful because of migration out, the incremental ideas that Turner and Elemental used in new builds can be applied to the preservation and reuse of buildings.

In the Denny Row project in Pittsburgh, featured in Chapter 6, the Allegheny West Civic Council invested $500,000 to rehabilitate the exteriors of a row of townhouses and then sold them as shells (with unfinished interiors) to individual buyers.[13] The architects who were engaged for the project produced an exterior-only drawing set. This half-house or incremental method reduced the purchase price for the buyers and, depending on their financing, allowed the residents to finish them out over time. The consolidated core concept, an example of which architecture graduate students developed, fabricated, and inserted into a historic house in Houston, profiled in Chapter 10, is another way that architects can use an incremental concept in redeveloping existing buildings.

Temporary occupancy can also be considered an incremental intervention. Entremise, an organization based in Montréal (Québec, Canada) has been studying, facilitating, and advocating for temporary use of vacant spaces since 2016. There are multiple benefits of temporary occupancy to underused buildings and disinvested communities, which are discussed more thoroughly in Chapter 6. Building professionals, sometimes in partnership with advocacy organizations such as Entremise, are engaged to navigate the permitting process for temporary use. The structural brace at Kilve Chantry in England (profiled in Chapter 4) was an incremental solution that addressed only part of the structure and facilitated adjacent use until a more permanent repair was put in place.

At a community scale, the iterative process focuses on implementing or prototyping ideas for improving the built environment that scale slowly over time, which can be guided by community values that are identified in or emergent from the inventory process (see Chapter 2). In the nineteenth century, Scottish town planner Patrick Geddes cautioned against the powerful new town planning movements that were coming into vogue at that time (precursors to the urban renewal movement), calling them "sweeping clearances."[14] Geddes argued instead for what he called "constructive and conservative surgery,"[15] favoring smaller interventions in the city. Prototyping is an example of these smaller iterative interventions.

Les Grands Voisins, a temporary use experiment that ran for five years in Paris, involved multiple interventions in existing buildings and open spaces within the areas around a vacant hospital complex (described further in Chapter 6). The time frame allowed the project organizers and city planners to identify which interventions were working well and to adapt and experiment when an intervention needed improvement. This small-scale experimentation and iteration is very valuable, particularly when attempting to reanimate underused buildings.

Learning from experimentation is the focus of the tactical urbanism movement.[16] This movement emphasizes the ways in which residents or municipalities can prototype solutions to gather feedback about how the solutions are working before major investments. For example, if considering turning a portion of a parking lot into a gathering place, tactical urbanism advocates prototype the solution through inexpensive, reversible means—such as traffic barricades and temporary market tents in the parking lot—to see how it works in real time, then make adjustments based on observations and feedback from users about the prototype. Documenting a prototype project is an important step in an effective process.

Sometimes resident-initiated changes can challenge the municipal status quo. In the best cases, the places where interventions run up against existing or broken systems can prompt positive change. For example, frustrated with repeated attempts to get the city to replace a missing stop sign at an intersection, Sweet Water Foundation founder Emmanuel Pratt created his own stop sign and mounted it at the problem intersection. When the City of Chicago issued a citation for the illegally placed sign, community insistence resulted in three new stop signs for the neighborhood.[17] The Heidelberg Project in Detroit, profiled in Chapter 5, was twice the subject of city-initiated demolitions in the 1990s but received municipal approval in 2022 for the project's signature polka dots painted on the street.[18] Experimental changes made in real space can demonstrate value. Sometimes reactions to unconventional interventions can change over time.

The stop sign in place, with the Thought Barn visible in the background, 2020. (Courtesy of Sweet Water Foundation)

Architects and others can be involved in helping to test and evaluate small plans and tactical responses. Oliver Wainwright's profile of Assemble Studio describes that when the architects were trying to help envision solutions to reinvigorating a town square, "they took up residence in an old kiosk on the town square and staged community events during a number of weeks, as full-scale tests for how the public realm might be improved. After orchestrating such things as a stage for pensioners' tea dances and ramps for young skateboarders, and reorganising the market, they proposed permanent improvements along similar lines. The result is a low-key collage of pieces that have since taken on a life of their own."[19]

Susan Ross, an architect and academic who works in sustainable heritage planning and conservation, points out that heritage reclamation projects often begin with a single living unit because smaller units of investment are lower risk and have different code and permitting requirements than larger or public structures.[20] My follow-on observation is that even though a larger building may be prioritized by the community as important to save, the larger project may be enabled and sustained by the completion of smaller projects in the neighborhood first.

Joseph Beuys's notion of social sculpture or increased cultural and creative action begins with one creative action and can grow incrementally, a "snowball effect," which architect and urban designer Matteo Robiglio observes as the "capability of attracting forces and gaining momentum while running."[21] This will be seen in many of the profiles in Part III, especially as the values or ideas behind the project are reinforced, precipitating more action and inviting more rings of community.

Alternatives for Financing and Delivering Professional Services

As discussed in Chapter 1, most modern architecture and preservation projects have a triangular structure of participants: the professional, the client, and the municipality. Funding drives the project through a series of personal, financial, and regulatory transactions to achieve the vision for the project. The professionals are paid a fee that is based roughly on the construction cost of the finished project. Most large projects are financed by credit, which can be elusive in neighborhoods considered high risk. Furthermore, this system of compensation and delivery favors the all-at-once (total completion of a project) rather than an incremental process.

Once a concept or project has proven itself, nonprofits, capacity building, and heritage advocacy organizations often come on board to fund them, but sometimes clients need something to move them toward these seed funds. How can architects provide services to help jump start a project or take it to the next iteration?

Although legality varies by location, structuring a professional service firm as a nonprofit is one way that professionals can work with disinvested communities within the established method of project delivery.[22] Using the mechanisms of redirected profits or donated funds, professionals pay themselves to provide their usual services for projects that may not otherwise have initial funding. Two well-known examples are Environmental Works in Seattle (Washington, US), which was founded in 1970, and Model of Architecture Serving Society (MASS) Design Group in Boston (Massachusetts, US), founded in 2007. Environmental Works has a Community Design Fund that allows the firm to offer no-fee design workshops to nonprofit clients. MASS created a Catalyst Fund for early efforts, allowing "mission-driven clients to start a project before they have the funds to build, after which point they should have the funds to pay the architect."[23]

Another approach is for professionals to donate their services. A 2022 publication by the American Institute of Architects titled "Architect's Role in Creating Equitable Communities" points out that larger, more established firms have more margin to offer pro bono services.[24] Smaller firms and individual practitioners may have less overhead margin but have the advantage of more flexibility. Some larger firms take a role in research, which is another way of serving the public and advancing knowledge about building reuse. For example, ERA, a conservation-focused architecture and planning firm based in Toronto (Ontario, Canada), has been undertaking research on tower renewal since the early 2000s.[25] Tower Renewal aims to develop strategies for transitioning existing high-rise housing buildings into more sustainable and resilient places.[26]

Pro bono services can also be organized collectively instead of on a firm-by-firm basis. Architects sans Frontières, which operates from Montréal (Québec, Canada), brings together architects and design professionals in ad hoc volunteer groups around one project at a time. Beginning in the early 2000s, there was a resurgent call for architects and designers to better connect with the needs of all members of society. The Cooper Hewitt National Design Museum's exhibits and publications *Design for the Other 90%* (2007) and

Design with the Other 90%: Cities (2011)[27] resonated with many professionals and students affiliated with groups such as Architecture for Humanity, who were concerned about the way that the current method of project delivery made architectural services available to only a privileged segment of society. Preservation-focused service groups such as HistoriCorps provide volunteer opportunities and skill training in historic preservation trades.

Academic-allied community design centers such as the Detroit Collaborative Design Center at the University of Detroit Mercy, cityLAB at the University of California Los Angeles, and the Rural Studio at Auburn University have a long history of standing in the gap for professional services within disinvested communities.

Compensating work also becomes more feasible when architects are involved on an episodic or as-needed basis. I remember some innovative architects in Hamtramck, Michigan—a small city within the city of Detroit—who set up in a storefront and had a walkup counter with minimal set fees for consultation. Although it is perhaps smaller in scope, the professional can view episodic involvement as an enlarged way of practicing.

Open conversations about service scopes, limits, and expectations help establish joint understanding.[28] In collaboration, professionals and community members can find creative ways to finance professional services and acknowledge contributions.

Considering Historic Preservation Standards and Designation

In the article "On Preservation: Heritage, History, and Exclusion," architect Susan Nigra Snyder writes about how historic district designation can serve as a tool for exclusion. "By making identify of place static, preservation provides the certainty that forces real-estate value," she argues. "A closer look at historic districts reveals that preservation comes at the expense of social, cultural, economic, and political diversity—and opportunity."[29] In contrast, Snyder says, "Progressive places are not bounded; they are porous, accepting new people and material change."[30]

A district (a street, several blocks, or a neighborhood) may be designated as historic by the local municipality, which means that exterior changes on structures in the district are reviewed and regulated. This overlay, intended to protect the historic integrity and preserve the character of the contributing structures, has socioeconomic implications beyond the structures. Many fear that a historic district designation will cause gentrification.

Although none of the neighborhoods profiled in Part III are historic districts, some buildings within the neighborhoods are historically designated or landmarked. I think that these communities and profiles demonstrate that it is important to designate some buildings and that neighborhoods and sites can co-host radically different approaches and scales to preservation and to reimagining existing buildings.

As discussed in Chapter 1, the historic preservation field is expanding discussions about how places are designated and what or whom a designation would benefit. In recent decades there has been movement toward values-based conservation, commemorating difficult stories that need to be acknowledged and finding ways to protect historic structures while maintaining diversity and the quirkiness that can characterize a community. Community land trusts, co-ops, rent or sale-price restrictions, and conservation districts are just some of the available tools and strategies.

There are no easy answers, and there is no formula. But the idea of maintaining porosity, to use Snyder's term, can be helpful. A community must consider change and how applied districts or designations will serve as a filter for future neighborhood composition—in terms of the physicality of the neighborhood and its demographics. Although rehabilitating buildings has potential to play a role in gentrification, I view extensive demolition of buildings as narrowing future options rather than expanding them. These same buildings can be generous resources for creativity and revitalization.

As standards evolve and the discussion continues around flexibility and the need to take a holistic community view, perhaps more episodic professional and municipal consultations could align with the incremental and iterative process in a struggling or revitalizing neighborhood. Jane Jacobs said, "Genuine, rich diversity of the built environment is always the product of many, many different minds, and at its richest is also the product of different periods of time with their different aims and fashions. Diversity is a small-scale phenomenon. It requires collections of little plans."[31]

The Granby Workshop is an enterprise that arose out of the collaboration between the Granby 4 Streets Community Land Trust and Assemble Studio, as described in Chapter 9. In the workshop, a sign announces the "rules" for the making of products. These include inviting chance and improvisation,

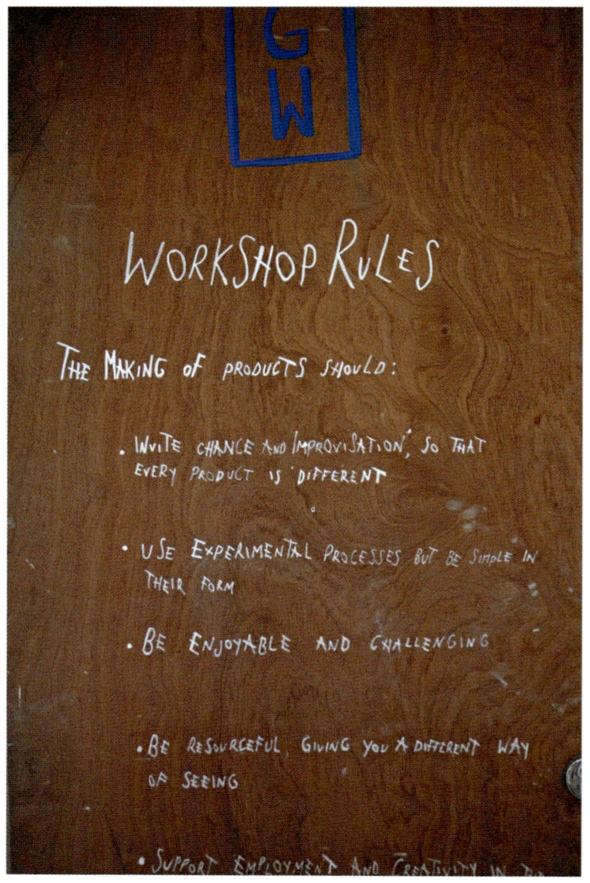

The Granby Workshop rules for their artistic products and process echo the spirit of community redevelopment in Granby, 2017. (Gary Calton)

using experimental processes, and being resourceful. I observe that these same "rules," which are meant for the creation of handcrafts in the workshop, also broadly describe the values that drove the approach to the renovation of the 10 Houses on Cairns and the Granby Winter Garden. Building on Snyder's concept of porosity, which implies a sort of filter, I wonder how communities could be in dialogue with broader regulating structures about different types and levels of filters. For example, if one of the filters selected was resourcefulness, discussions would center on questions such as "How does this proposed building intervention reinforce or support resourcefulness in our neighborhood?"

Part II is a catalog of the three approaches outlined in Chapter 2 (priority, prosaic, and poetic), featuring examples of each approach in sites around the world. Not all the sites are located in what could be described as disinvested communities, but they illustrate an idea or technique that can be useful in a disinvested context.

The approaches are not organized, like the Secretary of the Interior's Standards, according to intervention level. Rather, they're grouped according to the building's or site's purpose or role in the community. This method of organization is an attempt to move the focus away from the brick-and-mortar architecture of the building and its level of integrity and take the idea of integrity more broadly, as a building's cooperation as a unit within a community. A building is an object—but it's an object that's activated by its community, and its value is in its service to the community, even when it is only partially, temporarily, or very unconventionally reused.

Describing Assemble Studio's approach to working with communities as collaborators, *Guardian* writer Nate Berg says that the result is "temporary and permanent projects that simultaneously add to the built environment and fill a need within the community."[32] As artists, activists, residents, and built environment professionals invest in collective action that is both generative and generous, hope extends an arrow into the future. Collective actions on existing structures can build economic, social, and creative capital over time in a community-centered process that fuels further projects, ignites creativity, and speaks to all of us about our social history and relationship with place.

PART II

Purposeful Approaches to Existing Buildings

Charles Sheeler's painting of a domestic interior features both stairways and shadows: the shadows of our yesterdays and the stairways toward our tomorrows. Sometimes, as in this painting, they converge. (Charles Sheeler, *Home, Sweet Home*, 1931, oil on canvas. Detroit Institute of Arts, Gift of Robert H. Tannahill, 45.455)

Chapter 4

Priorities: Saving Endangered or Threatened Buildings

"My mind's troubled by some things that was spoken about yesterday," she said.

"We'll get to it when we're done with what's ahead."

—James McBride,
The Heaven and Earth Grocery Store

Sometimes a building is at the critical juncture of yesterday and tomorrow. The building may represent something significant in the community's past, whether troubling or triumphant. And although there may not be a clear path ahead, a skyward-reaching Jacob's ladder like the chair rungs in Sheeler's painting, the time has come for the building's community to choose: continuance or loss.

Priority repairs for a distressed building can make the difference between a building saved and a building lost. When communities rally around supporting or preserving an endangered structure, it is a powerful gesture. In this sense, prioritized repairs are the purest form of preservation—an action undertaken for the benefit of the future—and therefore an act of deepest

"My wish for you Is that you continue."
—Maya Angelou

faith. They are a declaration of the value of an at-risk building to the community and of hope for the future. As stated in Chapter 2, the priority approach is about choosing continuance. Maya Angelou's poem "Continue" contains the powerful lines "My wish for you / Is that you continue."[1]

When a building faces the threat of direct demolition or demolition by neglect, choosing to support and set aside that building for the future is a powerful act of resistance.

A priority repair—a temporary roof, a structural brace, or a board-up—becomes a visual symbol of resistance. These repairs directly resist the natural forces of gravity and water and the socioeconomic factors behind the building's deterioration, expressing a visual defiance. This resistance is an inherently hopeful action. Author Elin Kelsey defines hope as "an action that you do rather than a feeling that you have."[2] Because the number of at-risk buildings in a disinvested community is high, the approach of priority repairs assumes an inventory (see Chapter 2). Not all buildings can be saved, and not all are good candidates to be saved, so residents and community groups can rely on their inventory to direct their efforts. This inventory, in essence, is the first level triage. Once a building or buildings are identified, priority repairs are the next-level triage. Priority repairs address the most serious wounds on the building—the wounds that threaten the life of the building.

Priority repairs are an excellent opportunity to work with an architect or a building professional such as a structural engineer on a defined scope of work because of the technical nature of the repairs. The defined scope of work can also help with fundraising efforts because it offers focused opportunities for partnerships. The Society for the Protection of Ancient Buildings in the United Kingdom was one of the funders of the temporary structural brace for the Chantry at Kilve, profiled in this chapter.[3] A local masonry organization donated services for the Mullanphy building in St. Louis, also profiled in this chapter.

The two most common causes of damage necessitating priority repairs are roof leaks and structural instability. The integrity of the roof is crucial to conserving any building for future use. When the watertightness of the roof membrane or system is compromised, moisture penetrates other areas of the building, and the damage can be widespread. Roof leaks often lead to structural instability, as building materials deteriorate from weather damage.

If the roof is no longer effective and cannot be reasonably repaired, temporary roof options or enclosures can protect the structure beneath. These approaches are superstructures that float above the existing roof or remaining structure. There are myriad examples of protective roof structures and enclosures from which communities can draw ideas. At the Casa Grande site in Arizona (US), a roof superstructure protects ruins from deterioration. The first roof was installed at the site in 1903.[4]

In the early 1990s, I once walked into what appeared to be a large new industrial prefabricated shed in one of the US Great Plains states, to find a completely intact early nineteenth century one-room church inside. New meeting areas were simply arranged around this original church, like old-fashioned Sunday school picnics in its yard, within the enclosure of the new steel structure. It was a strange disjunction, but it was also a creative way that the congregation chose to preserve the original church while expanding its capacity. Shed roof canopies built over flat-roofed mobile homes are another vernacular example of protecting the structure beneath from water damage. The Menokin ruins, profiled in Chapter 8, have been protected for more than two decades by a metal roof canopy.

Two sites profiled in this chapter—the Chantry at Kilve and the Mullanphy building—received priority repairs to counteract structural instability. A structure can become unstable due to damage from fire or from elements such as water and wind after a period of vacancy or from a natural disaster. Seismic reinforcing may be needed to prevent earthquake damage. Temporary structural bracing prevents collapse while the future of the building is determined and funds are sourced for more extensive restorations.

A third type of priority repair discussed in this chapter is mothballing. If roof coverings and structural bracings are like medical triage, mothballing is like putting the building in a medically induced coma. In architecture, *mothballing* has evolved as a term to describe the process of preparing a building for a period of vacancy or disuse. It is the planned closure and active decommissioning of a building. Mothballing a building usually involves shutting off the utilities (water, electricity, gas), draining existing water and frostproofing the plumbing system, and ensuring adequate ventilation.

In preparation for a period of disuse, vandal-proof coverings are often installed on the doors and windows, and valuable or fragile items may be removed from the premises. The historic homes of Springfield in Jacksonville,

Florida, profiled in this chapter, were mothballed through efforts by members of a neighborhood preservation organization who believed that the homes were valuable to the future of their neighborhood, although it wasn't clear how future restorations would be funded.

Another priority strategy discussed in this chapter is documentation. Documentation is a valuable action for buildings or sites that are in a precarious state or have an uncertain outcome. In some cases, the documentation ends up being a record of something lost. In other cases, such as Menokin, it can guide preservation efforts in a period of action after the uncertain years.

In Central Europe, a collective of architects and artists called Abandoned (re)creation has been working to highlight the architectural treasures of the spa culture that have been abandoned in the decades since the transition in power in 1989 known as the Velvet Revolution.

Spa towns were built up during the Austro-Hungarian Empire and in the early days of Czechoslovakia after World War I, but many spa towns in the region also have notable buildings from the later modernist and brutalist periods. These spas, often historically situated near natural springs, were places of rejuvenation. Patrons were prescribed an individualized daily health regimen, but community was also a big part of the experience. People often visited the spa at the same time year after year, so networks of spa friendships formed. Spa culture was socially integral to health, vacationing, and community.

Abandoned (re)creation began organizing social and artistic activities to draw attention to the plight of these significant monuments. They mapped their conditions and researched their histories, eventually publishing two monographs and a film dedicated to spa architecture. Oral history was an important part of the documentation process. The group interviewed people who worked at the spas and people who frequented the spas to underscore not only the architecture but also the unique culture it fostered. It was an atmosphere that eventually few will be left to remember.

The Machnáč Sanatorium Spa in Trenčianske Teplice, Slovakia, is considered one of the most significant representatives of European functionalism from Czechoslovakia in the period between World War I and World War II and was listed on the national heritage register in 1969. Designed by architect Jaromír Krejcar, the spa building, which was completed in 1932, was a vision of avant-garde modernism, integrated technology, and social progress.

Historic photo of Machnáč Sanatorium, circa late 1930s. (Archive of Abandoned (re) creation/Andrea Kalinová, Martin Zaiček)

Machnáč Sanatorium exterior, 2018. (Archive of Abandoned (re) creation/Andrea Kalinová, Martin Zaiček)

Machnáč is a *t*-shaped building with common spaces including a cafeteria and reading room, open roof terraces, and patient rooms with individual balconies. The concrete structure has horizontal ribbons of glass that are, in many cases, sliding and folding windows that connect the interior to the building's park setting. After a period of decline in use, the spa was abandoned in 2002.

For the activity named "Room 106," Abandoned (re)creation used archival documentation to guide a one-day installation in a guest room at the Machnáč Spa. They installed flooring, painted the walls and balcony, and added coordinated cushions and period furnishings. The installation was a glimpse of the past, a time-travel to the period when the spa was welcoming visitors into its bright corridors. But the necessarily temporary nature of

Room 106 before installation, 2014. (Archive of Abandoned (re)creation/Andrea Kalinová, Martin Zaiček)

the installation (as it was unpermitted) also highlighted the distance between what the space was, what it is, and the still-open-ended question of what it will be in the future.

Abandoned (re)creation's installations and their attention to documentation are examples of priority approaches. In the film she created about the abandoned Machnáč Spa, Andrea Kalinová asks, "Which is dysfunctional: the building or the society?" By occupying and documenting various dimensions of the vacated spaces, both physical and social, Abandoned (re)creation offers an invitation into the complex collective process of re-creating.[5]

The past can be tangle of troubles that is difficult to unravel. It can loom large in the daily lives of individuals and communities, a pall cast on the present. But actions in the present are also continually shaping the future.

Room 106 during installation, 2014. (Archive of Abandoned (re)creation/Andrea Kalinová, Martin Zaiček)

When a building reaches a critical juncture, such as the threat of demolition or the danger of impending collapse, this juncture is a pinpoint where priorities shape a response.

In this chapter, the example projects are titled according to the architectural technique that they demonstrate (as opposed to the purpose or benefit by which they are titled in later chapters). This is because all the case studies in this chapter have a similar purpose: to keep the building around. Although not all the case studies featured in this chapter are in disinvested communities, they demonstrate techniques or processes that can be useful for retaining buildings in a disinvested context.

Retaining an at-risk building through the priority approach is an acknowledgment of the full history of the building and the community over time. Accepting some deterioration, damage, and periods of disuse and uncertainty are part of continuance. In times of distress, crisis, or loss, the choices communities make about their buildings shape the telling of their future.

Stabilization: Mullanphy Emigrant Home (St. Louis, Missouri, US)

In 2007, St. Louis weekly newspaper *The Riverfront Times* named the Mullanphy Emigrant Home the "best lost cause of the year."[6] It was a prescient pronouncement. The building was destroyed by fire in 2023, during the writing of this book. It's much more lost now than it was then, and it seems as though its final time of death has been called. I struggled with whether to keep this case study in the collection, and yet I'll lead with it because its eulogy contains, in equal measure, hope and heartbreak.

The Italianate building, built in 1867, was designed by architects George Barnett and Albert Piquenard as a dormitory for immigrants. The dormitory construction was funded by the estate of Bryan Mullanphy, St. Louis's tenth mayor. Mullanphy, the son of an Irish immigrant, specified that one third of his estate be used to "provide relief to all poor emigrants passing through St. Louis to settle in the West."[7]

As pointed out by building researcher Chris Naffziger in a profile on the building, the Mullanphy's sturdy classical architecture reflected a reformer's belief that "august architecture could influence a building's inhabitants, making them more moral and upright citizens in the process."[8] The dormitory housed primarily European immigrants who were disembarking

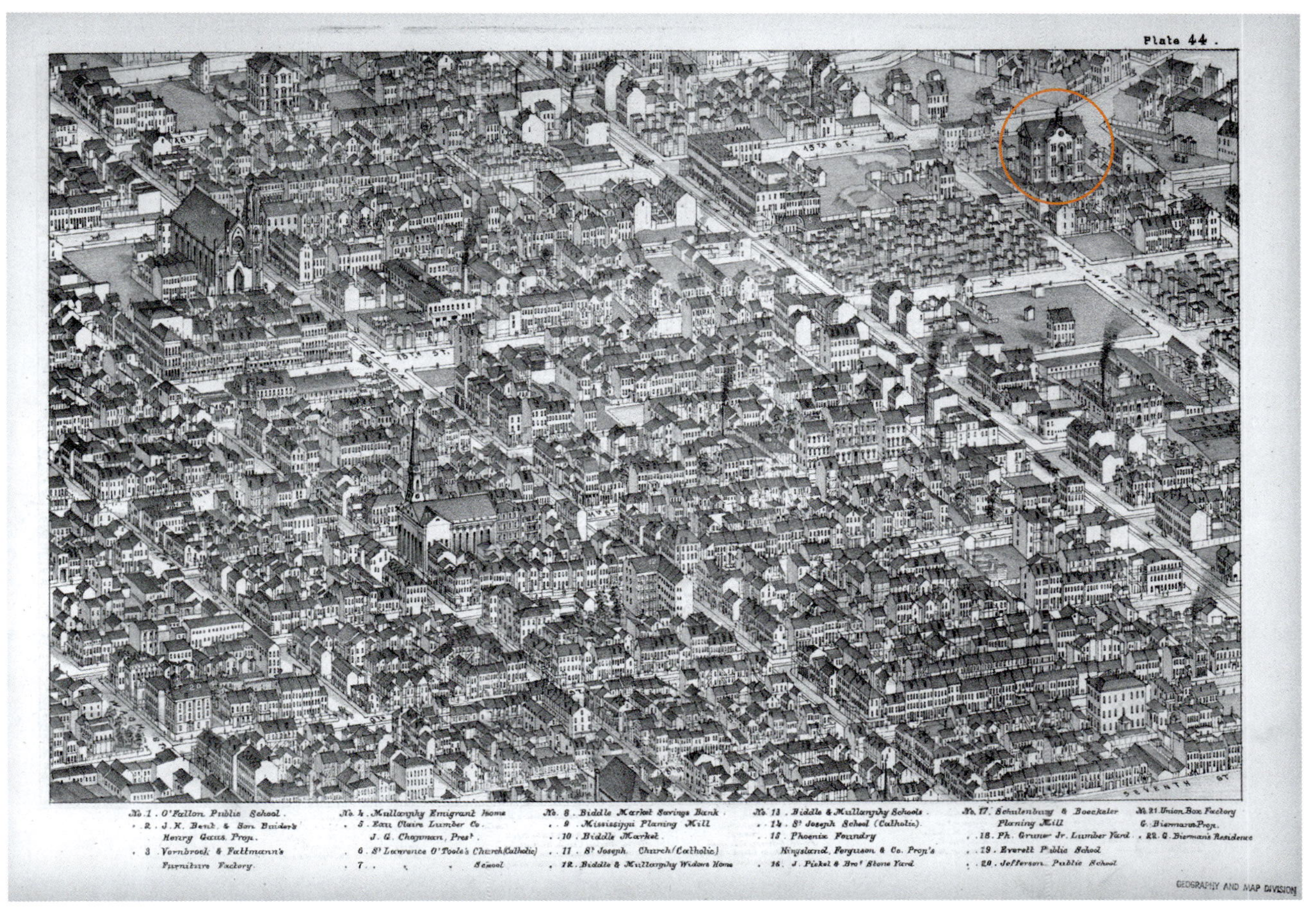

A pictorial mcp of St. Louis, with the Mullanphy bu lding in the upper right corner, 1876. (Richard J. Compton and Camille N. Dry. Pictorial St. Louis, the great metropolis of the Mississippi Valley; a topographical survey drawn in perspective A.D. St. Louis, Compton & Co., 1876. Map. Plate 44. Library of Congress Geography and Map Division [Call number G1439.S4 C6 1876. Control number rc01001392])

daily from the steamboats on the Mississippi River, providing room and board for them until they found employment or continued their onward journey.

Even before the building's completion, doubts were raised about its design. An 1867 article in the *Missouri Republican* commented on the proposed arrangement of the upper floors: "When the building is crowded with immigrants, male and female, it would seem as if the arrangement of the larger apartments will hardly be conducive to cleanliness or morality."[9]

Within a decade of its construction, the building was sold and converted for use as a factory. The Absorene Company, which purchased the building, manufactured wallpaper and book cleaner in the space. Under the ownership of Absorene, much of the building's original ornamentation was removed.

The cupola was dismantled and the high, scrolled pediment was simplified to a triangular shape.

Part of the building's history is a link to the broader story of migration and westward expansion in the United States. (A banner created by the Old North St. Louis Restoration Group, advocating for the building's preservation stated, "A century before there was an Arch, this was the Gateway to the West."[10]) The building's history also speaks to industrialization and urban morphology, disinvestment, and demolition. The account of the district discussed in the National Register of Historic Places Nomination Form in 1982 parallels many of the broader sociological forces discussed in Chapter 1:

> The Mullanphy District was scheduled for total demolition and industrial expansion. The first "slum clearance" had begun in 1940 for nearby 1,658-unit Carr Square Village Public Housing. Large-scale, Federally funded public housing projects after World War II cleared vast areas between Cass Avenue and the edge of Downtown; Interstate 70 obliterated links to the Mississippi River. . . . St. Louis experienced almost a decade of demolition by neglect and intent between 1964 and 1974, . . . [and later,] "War on Poverty" programs . . . took precedence over non-funded preservation efforts in an area increasingly deemed dangerous. The first professional architectural survey was not conducted until 1978 after the nationally televised demolition of the fifty acre Pruitt-Igoe Public Housing complex just blocks away.[11]

The Mullanphy building continued to serve as a factory through the 1980s, after which it was abandoned. In the spring of 2006, a series of storms caused the collapse of the entire south wall of the three-story masonry structure.

Temporary shoring in the gaping hole of the south wall probably amplified the damage that resulted from a second storm by creating a wind tunnel effect that took out parts of the east and north walls. The building department advocated immediate emergency demolition. The St. Louis Landmarks Association cited the building on its "Most Endangered" list. There was a sense of urgency within the local community and the preservation community, who rallied around the building. Thanks to a well-coordinated effort, it was eventually acquired by a local nonprofit, the Old North St. Louis Restoration Group, late in 2007.

Mullanphy building, 2005. (Michael R. Allen)

Mullanphy building, 2007. (Michael R. Allen)

Mullanphy building, 2008. (Michael R. Allen)

Mullanphy door detail, circa 2008. (Michael R. Allen)

Old North coordinated the preparation of architectural plans and solicited donations of labor and materials from the Masonry Contractors Association. A masonry contracting firm came forward to oversee the repairs on a pro-bono basis and shortly thereafter, the stabilization of the south side of the building with a concrete masonry unit backup wall was completed.

In 2018, the building was sold to a new owner who, as an immigrant himself, felt a connection to the history of the building and pledged to preserve its legacy.[12] Yet, there remained funding gaps, which only increased after third collapse at the site brought renovation costs even higher. Five years later, on September 14, 2023, a fire destroyed the building and demolition began within a few days.

Architectural historian Michael Allen, who chronicled the Mullanphy for many years, points out that if a new roof had been installed on the building in the years after the stabilization effort, the building would perhaps still be standing, because more recent collapses could have been prevented. "Water was getting into the west wall," he notes, "because there was no drip edge and no gutter to carry it away."[13]

Mullanphy building, 2023. (Michael R. Allen)

Allen salvaged some remnants of the building, which are now in the collection of the National Building Museum in Washington, DC, 2023. (Michael R. Allen)

The Mullanphy Emigrant Home history demonstrates the importance of prioritizing emergency repairs and monitoring the building, and the concurrent importance of community engagement. Community engagement was probably highest during the campaign by Old North, which coordinated sustained conversations with the city, students, neighbors, consultants, and preservation organizations. Could a temporary use have helped activate the building during these years?

It's sad to see a substantial building reduced to rubble, especially one that survived decades of urban demolition and has been the focus of so many prioritization and preservation efforts over the years. Its remnants carry these stories together, lessons and loss.

Bricks spilling out the door of the Mullanphy building after the fire in September 2023. (Jackie Dana. Unseen St. Louis)

Structural Support: Chantry at Kilve (Kilve, Somerset, UK)

Kilve is a tiny seaside village in England, recorded in the 1086 Domesday book as Clive.[14] The village's economy rests in part on tourism, and the historic area includes a fourteenth century chantry (a chapel). Kilve Chantry is attached to a manor house that was the home for the de Furneaux family throughout the fourteenth century. In 1329, Sir Simon de Furneaux founded the chantry for five priests to pray for his soul "in Kylve church."[15] The chantry is constructed of blue lias stone, a locally quarried stone consisting of limestone and shale layers.

Although the chantry fell into disrepair in the centuries that have passed since its construction, the structure remained in use as a barn and possibly as a cache or drop point for brandy smugglers until a fire around 1850.[16] The fire gutted the building, leaving only ruins. Over decades, exposure to the elements increased deterioration. For a time, it was listed in the category of "immediate risk of further rapid deterioration" on English Heritage's "Heritage at Risk" register.[17]

Danger sign at Chantry Cottage, Kilve, 2002. (© Historic England Archive)

Given the precarious state of the structure, heritage organizations funded a series of emergency repairs in the early 2000s. One of these repairs was a steel structural brace applied to the back of the chantry end wall, which was leaning precariously. The brace, designed by engineer Patrick Stow, was set on pins that included load cells to measure the load being carried by the frame, which increased over time as the wall leaned into the supports.[18] Although the project design brief specified a short-term solution, Patrick Stow designed the intervention with a minimum twenty-five-year design life. "I decided to go for something eye-catching and long lasting as I recognised that the fund raising for the masonry repairs would take many years to achieve a result," said Patrick Stow.[19]

Brace from the side showing the extent of lean of the gable wall onto the frame, now load bearing, 2005. (Photo by Patrick Stow)

Indeed, nearly twenty years later, masonry consolidation combined with structural tiebacks to a new floor structure finally allowed the brace to be removed. For those twenty years between, this essential repair kept the structure upright and supported use of an adjacent space as a tea garden and heritage attraction for the village of Kilve.

William Wordsworth mentions Kilve in his poem "Anecdote for Fathers," published in 1798. The poem contrasts the formal reasoning of an adult with the simple perspective of a child. The father asks his child whether he would rather be at Kilve, on the seaside, or at Liswyn farm, where they are walking.

The tea garden adjacent to the Chantry walls, 2017. (Getty Images / Stephen Dorey)

The child answers that he would rather be at Kilve, and when pressed he explains his preference in the following way:

> Then did the boy his tongue unlock,
> And eased his mind with this reply:
> "At Kilve there was no weather-cock;
> And that's the reason why."

One reading of the poem is that the boy preferred Kilve because at Kilve, the boy need only feel or experience which way the wind was blowing without an instrument to tell him. It is this directness of experience that Wordsworth praised. A direct and simple analogy was what Patrick Stow had in mind in designing the brace, with an anthropomorphic wink. The top story window opening is the head, the arms support the columns on each side of the doorway, and the legs of the brace are splayed out as they push the structure upright.[20]

Brace view from the front to show "Kilve Man" imagery, 2005. (Photo by Patrick Stow)

Elevated view of the Chantry, Kilve, from the southeast, showing completed grant-aided repairs, 2022. (© Historic England Archive)

The structural brace at the Chantry at Kilve expressed a directness of experience. The wall was trying to collapse. The brace held it up. There is no weather cock to tell us about the winds of these walls' future. But now, thanks to twenty years of "temporary" bracing and the recent, more extensive repairs, they stand.

Mothballing: Homes of Springfield District (Jacksonville, Florida, US)

After a fire consumed over two thousand buildings in central Jacksonville in 1901, many residents relocated to the newly forming Springfield district on the North Side of Jacksonville. The homes constructed in this district are primarily one- and two-story wood frame structures that reflect the vernacular architectural styles of the early twentieth century in the United States: Queen Anne, Prairie, and colonial revivals. It's a typical walkable residential community from this time period: an orthogonal street grid dotted with civic buildings such as churches and schools and a small commercial area.

The Springfield district was added to the National Register of Historic Places in 1987. Yet even at the time of the historic designation report, the neighborhood was experiencing some abandonment and distress. Historic designation at the national level can offer incentive for investment through tax credits, but it is often powerless to prevent demolition if a structure is a difficult candidate for investment. Furthermore, as disinvestment continues, demolition by neglect occurs when owners do not have the resources to maintain the building or do not choose to because of diminished property values.

In Springfield's case, the abandonment and disinvestment eventually prompted demolitions. The grassroots group Preservation SOS (Save Our Springfield) was formed in 2010 as a response to these demolitions. Recognizing that once a building is demolished, the resource is lost to the community, Preservation SOS advocated for a mothballing program in the historic district. Mothballing is an effective priority strategy because it doesn't require a known future use. It is quite simply an effort to keep the building around.

The program put forth by the grassroots effort was a Mothballing Certificate of Appropriateness, or Mothballing COA, which is a certificate given to a structure by the municipality. According to the Jacksonville legislation, passed in 2011, the priorities of mothballing are to stabilize the structure and prevent it from becoming unsafe; to establish monitoring and maintenance criteria; and to ensure that the structure will not detrimentally affect nearby properties but will contribute to larger community preservation goals.[21]

The Mothballing COA process offers several benefits to a historic building, its owner, and the community. First, it freezes fines for code violations, which had often led owners to simply demolish buildings to avoid mounting fines. Second, it secures and protects a building against further damage. Most importantly, the COA encourages the owner to work toward an eventual Certificate of Occupancy, even if it is a long-term goal. In Jacksonville, annual inspections are a requirement of the Mothballing COA. Once issued, the Mothballing COA is valid for three years, which may be extended.

Preservation SOS also created a way for owners to donate buildings to the group, which would help mobilize a volunteer base to obtain a Mothballing COA for the property. In all, fifteen houses were donated and only one has not yet been addressed. Two were sold, four were mothballed, and the remainder were given to members of the community.[22]

In 2012, the year after the legislation was passed, there were no demolitions in the district of Springfield for the first year since the district's historic

A Preservation SOS member tears up a demolition sign after a successful mothballing, 2011. (Photo by Preservation SOS)

Painting a boarded window sash on a mothballed house, 2012. (Photo by Preservation SOS)

designation in 1987.[23] This speaks to the effectiveness of the legislation and of the community mobilization efforts and countless volunteer hours of concerned neighbors.

Preservation SOS continues to engage the community on housing-related efforts with "Make It Happen" projects, such as gathering community volunteers to address maintenance needs requested by an elderly community member and paying back property taxes for another long-time resident.

An example of the community's success is the preservation of Dancy Terrace, a midblock bungalow court originally constructed in the early twentieth century. Eight of the twenty-four bungalows in the court have passed through

A Preservation SOS member shows the love for a mothballed house at Dancy Terrace, 2012. (Photo by Preservation SOS)

the hands of Preservation SOS, nineteen have been renovated, and the court's common spaces are now being maintained by a vested local property owner.

One of Preservation SOS's founders, Nicole Lopez, said, "Code enforcement is a bit scary because they say 'either you fix it or we take it down,' and there's never been an in-between."[24] Because of the in-between pathway of the Mothballing COA ordinance, sites that could have easily become empty lots through demolition are instead structures that contribute to the historic continuity of the community.

Dancy Terrace mothballing workday, 2012. (Photo by Preservation SOS)

Dancy Terrace, 2024. (Photo by Preservation SOS)

Protest and Documentation: Richard Nickel in Chicago (Chicago, Illinois, US)

The mid twentieth century was a turbulent period of urban change in Chicago, including rapid and widespread demolition of significant portions of the city fabric. These demolitions were fueled not only by urban renewal and highway-building projects, but also by a powerful consumerist culture of the shiny-new that prioritized the prospective over the existing. "Chicago in the impatient 1950s and 1960s," author Richard Cahan writes, "would not be concerned with coddling the past."[25]

Richard Nickel was an architectural photographer who dedicated his life to preserving the nineteenth-century structures that were being demolished in Chicago during this period. Nickel was a particular advocate of the work of

Protestors at the Chicago Stock Exchange (Chicago Stock Exchange Building, Adler & Sullivan, architects). Photo from 1971. A sign at the front states, "Only barbarians destroy great works of public art." (Richard Nickel Archive, Ryerson and Burnham Art and Architecture Archives, The Art Institute of Chicago. Digital File #201006_120214-019)

architectural firm Adler & Sullivan. Adler & Sullivan were among the leaders of the Chicago school of architecture in the late nineteenth century who were instrumental in developing the early technology and aesthetic vocabulary of the high rise.

Nickel's tactics for saving buildings from demolition were grassroots driven. He wrote letters, secured interviews, generated publicity, and participated in pickets. Nickel was also an active participant on Historic American Buildings Survey (HABS) teams as an architectural photographer. HABS is a documentation program for historic or significant structures in the United States, often initiated when a structure is considered at risk. During the HABS process, a publicly accessible archive is created that includes a historic report, measured drawings, and photographs. (HABS is also discussed in the profile of Menokin in Chapter 8.)

The images that Nickel captured for HABS document the form, proportions, and materiality of the buildings. Nickel also turned the lens of his Hasselblad camera toward building demolitions. These photographs convey much more raw emotion and drama, as Nickel captured at close hand the workers with saws hacking through the metal and stone. These images speak not only of material destruction and waste but also of the destruction of the city fabric and social continuity that the buildings represented.

It cannot be left unsaid that Nickel was a collector of architectural ornament. When a demolition was imminent, Nickel sometimes resorted to guerilla tactics to salvage ornaments from the buildings before they were gone. He amassed hundreds of architectural ornaments and in 1965, he sold part of his personal collection to Southern Illinois University, Edwardsville.[26] Many other pieces remained in his two-story storefront photography studio on Chicago's West Side.[27]

HABS-type documentation is noninvasive, but salvaging ornament from buildings brings with it many ethical questions. Some argue for the environmental merit of architectural salvage, while others question whether the market for salvage accelerates demolitions[28] or encourages theft. The next case study on moving buildings outlines some ethical questions related to the mobility of cultural resources and the topic merits more exploration, particularly in the context of disinvested communities.[29]

Nickel's swan song was the Chicago Stock Exchange building, a thirteen-story Adler & Sullivan structure built in 1893–1894. After a heated battle between the city and preservationists, the Stock Exchange was approved for

Photo of the Schiller Building (64 W. Randolph, Chicago) taken for HABS by Richard Nickel, 1961. Note the mascarons (representations of human heads) in this detail of the top story. (Library of Congress, Prints & Photographs Division, HABS, Reproduction number HABS ILL,16-CHIG,60—1)

demolition in 1972.[30] Nickel worked on the demolition site for as long as he could—documenting and reclaiming some of the pieces. Ultimately, it cost him his life. Twenty-six days after Nickel was reported missing, his body was recovered from the basement of the building. Author Richard Cahan later called Nickel "the conscience of the city."[31]

Documentation of threatened or lost structures can serve not only as a record, but also as a conscience. I'm reminded of a collage called *Public Execution* by William Allison Bostik, in the collection of the Detroit Institute of Arts. It's about the demolition of the former Detroit City Hall, which was con-

Removal of terracotta cornice ornament before demolition at the Chicago Stock Exchange (Chicago Stock Exchange Building, Adler & Sullivan, architects). Photo by Richard Nickel, circa 1972. (Richard Nickel Archive, Ryerson and Burnham Art and Architecture Archives, The Art Institute of Chicago. Digital File # 201006_110516-010)

structed in 1871 and demolished in 1961, despite preservationists' efforts to block the demolition through the courts. The collage's title invites the viewer to question the event it depicts: Was the public's will being executed through government, or was it merely a public execution of a building?

Most of these infamous demolitions—the Chicago Exchange, New York's Penn Station, the Detroit City Hall—were undertaken because of development pressure for new buildings. In disinvested communities, development pressure is less often the case. As discussed in Chapter 1, demolition is often

Demolition at the E. Rothschild and Brothers Store (E. Rothschild and Brothers Store, Dankmar Adler & Co., architects). Photo by Richard Nickel, 1972. (Richard Nickel Archive, Ryerson and Burnham Art and Architecture Archives, The Art Institute of Chicago. Digital File # 201006_191016-602)

viewed as a way of making a blank slate and clearing away problems that the buildings represent.

When a community identifies an important endangered building or site, documentation is a critical action that can be taken to record what is while envisioning what could be. Oral histories, such as those gathered for the Machnáč Spa, are an important companion to the documentation of a building's physical form. Although documentation is not a physical repair, it is categorized as a priority approach because it's a marker in time that has again and again proven invaluable further down the line.

As noted on the Library of Congress HABS collection page, "Buildings and engineering structures are large objects not easily maintained or preserved once they have outlived their functional or economic usefulness. Documentation

Richard Nickel locks eyes with a mascaron at the top of the Schiller Building (Schiller Building, Adler & Sullivan, architects) during its demolition. Photo from 1961. (Richard Nickel Archive, Ryerson and Burnham Art and Architecture Archives, The Art Institute of Chicago. Digital File # 201006_191016-669)

becomes an alternative means of preservation when demolition is inevitable. Documentation is also a primary tool for the stewardship of historic structures, whether for day-to-day care or as protection from catastrophic loss."[32] Documenting a building or site is like a community writing a letter to its future self. And to stand on the promise of that future is to stake a claim in hope.

Moving: Collected Thoughts and Examples

In French, buildings are called *immeubles* and furnishings are called *meubles*. I tend to think of these terms in English shorthand as "immovables" and "movables." But in some cases, the immovables (buildings) are movable. The Temple of Dendur, originally constructed in Nubia (now Egypt) in 10 BCE, was relocated to the Metropolitan Museum of the Arts in New York in the late 1960s because of the construction of the Aswan Dam.[33] At a different scale, Chapter 1 discussed how the White House, a single-family wood home, was relocated from Detroit to Europe on exhibit in 2016.

Relocation is something that the art world has been grappling with for years through ethical questions about the ownership of antiquities and discussions of art repatriation. Who owns cultural artifacts? How do we safeguard them and how do we share them? And although buildings seem to us to be static and immovable, our built environment is always changing. Ada Louise Huxtable, former architecture critic for *The New York Times*, declared "there is no art as impermanent as architecture."[34]

Detroit City Hall demolition, 1961. (Walter P. Reuther Library, Archives of Labor and Urban Affairs, Wayne State University. Detroit News Collection. [vmc_70789-2])

When the Mayor's Committee for the Preservation of Babe Ruth's Birthplace in Baltimore (Maryland, US) was considering dismantling and relocating the home of the baseball legend in the 1960s, Huxtable wrote a scathing article in the *Times*, saying "In urban terms, preservation is the saving of the essence and style of other eras, through their architecture and urban forms, so that the meaning and flavor of those other times and tastes are incorporated into the mainstream of the city's life. The accumulation is called culture."[35] Babe Ruth's birthplace was not moved, and its location later proved symbiotic with the construction of Oriole Park at Camden Yards in the early 1990s. This, of course, could not have been anticipated during the debate about the rowhouse at 216 Emory Street in the late 1960s.

Babe Ruth Birthplace and Museum, Baltimore, 2012. (Public domain. Smallbones, CC0, via Wikimedia Commons)

In Detroit, the relocation of the Gem Theatre for the construction of baseball stadium Comerica Park in the 1990s was a massive effort as the over 5-million-pound structure was moved approximately 300 feet a day. A decade prior, a dedicated coalition of a nonprofit, a citizen council, and their architects coordinated funding and logistics to move three homes onto Bagley Street in the nearby Corktown district of Detroit. The sites where the homes had been removed became surface parking for baseball venue Tiger Stadium, which was later torn down as obsolete and replaced by aforementioned Comerica Park.

I find the relocation of the Corktown homes to have been quite thoughtful. The architects developed a thorough analysis of the recipient lots and moving strategy, noting, "The program was not intended to 'pirate' nice little Victorian cottages from the surrounding area because they 'fit in' with the project area. They had to be houses that would otherwise be lost if not moved."[36] Today, the relocated homes, the adjacent homes of similar scale and era, and a mature tree canopy are a cohesive visual rhythm against which newer buildings of later periods are differentiated.

Moving the Gem Theatre, Detroit, 1997. (Walter P. Reuther Library, Archives of Labor and Urban Affairs, Wayne State University. Photo by Dale Rich. Dale Rich Collection. [rich_28053])

Gem Theatre, Detroit, with football arena Ford Field in the background, 2014. (Amy Hetletvedt)

In some cases moving a building or buildings has worked well in disinvested contexts, saving structures and benefiting communities. Chapter 10 describes how Project Row Houses (PRH) in Houston welcomed the Freedmen's shotgun houses, which were moved from an adjacent ward and are now part of PRH's arts and community programming.

Moving is a tool for disinvested communities to consider,[37] but there are crucial concerns about the strategy of moving buildings when approached

Fragments from other buildings (sometimes called spolia) have been incorporated into Chicago's Tribune Tower (constructed 1923–1925), including a brick from baseball stadium Comiskey Park. Photographed 2022. (Amy Hetletvedt)

from an equity perspective. A central issue of moving buildings is that there is a donor community and a recipient community. Moving may be a rescue, but it is also a removal. Or, as stated by a historic house-moving developer in the 1990s, "I may be stealing history, but I am also saving it."[38]

The recipient community can sometimes be enriched by receiving the building, but great consideration must be given to the effects on the donor community. Moving a building can easily become a means for further deresourcing an underresourced or disinvested community. As with demolition, moving can be hailed as a quick fix for a problem that may benefit from the latitude of time.

Two of the relocated houses: The Buzzard-Katz duplex (left) and the Simpson House (right) in the Corktown neighborhood of Detroit, 2024. (Amy Hetletvedt)

Bagley Street sidewalk view of the relocated houses in Corktown, 2024. (Amy Hetletvedt)

This work by Rona Pondick can be viewed as conveying a similar theme to Lucille Clifton's poem. The narrating mouth expresses a dark word bubble that contains an opposing mouth. Outside this word bubble, which resembles the form of a whale, floats a school of smaller fish, composed of the phrase "I want." The work invites consideration of how our own deep desires are minimized and obscured by the heavy narrative of another. [Rona Pondick (American, born 1952), *Mouth #46* 1994, casein, pigment, and graphite on mulberry paper, 32 × 47.9 cm (12 5/8 × 18 7/8 in.). Image courtesy the National Gallery of Art. Gift of Werner H. and Sarah-Ann Kramarsky, National Gallery of Art, Washington, 2000.41.18, and Image © Courtesy of Rona Pondick]

Chapter 5

The Poetic: Activating Buildings Through Narratives

"they ask me to remember

but they want me to remember

their memories

and i keep on remembering

mine."

—Lucille Clifton, "why some people be mad at me sometimes," from *How to Carry Water: Selected Poems*. Copyright © 1987 by Lucille Clifton. Reprinted with the permission of The Permissions Company, LLC on behalf of BOA Editions Ltd., boaeditions.org. From *Blessing the Boats* by Lucille Clifton, published by Penguin Classics. Copyright © Lucille Clifton, 2000. Reprinted by permission of Penguin Books Limited.

Activating buildings through narratives offers poetic beauty in the form of a visual commentary, which can powerfully represent communities and their stories. Buildings speak the history of a society and its values. Buildings that have been saved reflect the socioeconomic power structures that deemed them important. When disinvested or historically underrepresented communities save buildings that tell their stories, the scales tilt toward a more inclusive historical narrative. Providing critical perspective on a past event or current phenomenon honors the community from which these narratives hail.

The case studies in this chapter demonstrate how thoughtful building or site interventions might critique, illustrate, or illuminate broader phenomena such as migration, disinvestment, and inequality by making an aspect of brokenness more visible. Several of the case studies in this chapter were led by artists who used devices such as contrast or recontextualization to offer a critical perspective. What makes artists uniquely equipped to initiate these interventions? One reason is their cultivated practice of seeing and then calling a viewer to see something with them.

Recontextualizing objects and symbols was a prominent part of the artistic Dada movement that emerged during World War I, the most well-known example of which is Marcel Duchamps's *Fountain*. The "fountain" was a urinal, which he submitted to the Society of Independent Artists exhibit in New York in 1917. An off-the-shelf sanitary fixture proposed as art questions the meaning of art and making and questions what is collected and what is waste.

One way to recontextualize is to use buildings and sites as a full-scale collage, collecting and reusing objects from the community. Examples include the Magic Gardens, created by Isaiah Zagar in Philadelphia; Raymond Isidore's Maison Picassiette in Chartres, France; Simon Rodia's Watts Towers in Los Angeles; Olayami Dabls's Mbad African Bead Museum in Detroit; or Tyree Guyton's Heidelberg Project, also in Detroit, which is profiled in this chapter.

These artistic installations incorporate found objects and use structures as a canvas, contrasting at a fine, detailed, and meticulous scale the broader-scaled history of the site's surrounds. Maison Picassiette creator Raymond Isidore's work collapses the multigenerational construction of cathedrals and other famed structures—to which massive societal resources were dedicated—into a work completed within his own lifetime from discarded ceramics. Watts Tower creator Simon Rodia, whose life was roughly

Maison Picassiette, Chartres, France, 2022. (Amy Hetletvedt)

contemporaneous to Isidore's, created and adorned large-scale sculptures from environmental discards. The way the artists carefully bejeweled objects elevates the value of discards and the aspirations of citizen–creators who are often overlooked.

The very term *outsider art*, in which these creations are often categorized, acknowledges the simultaneous existence and creation of art and architecture that are inside the circle of sanction and laud and the art and architecture that are outside of it. Discussions of what we choose to preserve and how we choose to preserve it have cultural layers. At sites of global significance, there's often a negotiation of values between the local community, the government, and the international community about what is important to preserve, what counts as an archive, and how the history of the site is authenticated.

In the aftermath of the Coventry Blitz in World War II, one of the worst attacks on the British, the fourteenth-century gothic cathedral of St. Michael was in ruins. Instead of reconstructing the heavily damaged church, the community chose an alternative vision. As with St. Luke's Liverpool, which is profiled in this chapter, the Coventry community chose to leave the site as a ruin. At Coventry, provost Richard Howard guided the parishioners, theologically and psychologically, toward a remembrance that acknowledged the tragedy and made room for something new. Adjacent to the site of the ruins, a modern and architecturally divergent building was consecrated in 1962.

There are many examples of interventions built in, on, or alongside a ruin, at many different scales. In the dense urban environment of New York City, high-rises cluster around the void of the 9/11 Memorial, where two pools mark the site of the former twin towers and honor those lost in the attack. In Mississippi, the restored Ben Roy's Service Station, profiled in this chapter, can serve as a platform for viewing the adjacent ruins of the grocery that is part of the history of the murder of Emmett Till.

Sometimes, remembering forms the outlines of a void. It acknowledges the emptiness of something gone, the impossibility of retrieval. Franklin Court, designed by Venturi, Scott Brown, and Associates in 1976, is an outline or ghost of the house that Benjamin Franklin built for himself two centuries before, of which nothing remained. For a 2012 installation at the Art Institute of Chicago, artist Spencer Finch reproduced wallpaper from the hallway of the home of poet Emily Dickinson's brother Austin. The wallpaper

Coventry Cathedral, November 15, 1940, by John Piper (1903–1992), oil on plywood (Manchester Art Gallery, UK © Manchester Art Gallery/Bridgeman Images, © 2024 The Piper Estate/Artists Rights Society [ARS], New York/DACS, London)

is faded down its length, except for the squares where pictures once hung. Palimpsest (the installation title and a term for an object that retains traces of an earlier form) reminds us of the passage of time and reveals how even the slightest physical record can recall a past presence.

Sometimes a narrative structure is something new that echoes what was there before—not a reconstruction of a lost building but a new structure that remembers what was lost by reusing the materials or repeating the forms of the lost building. Wang Shu's Ningbo Museum (Ningbo, China) is one example of this. In what architectural historian Grace Ong Yan characterizes as a response to large-scale demolitions and reconstruction projects, the new building incorporated millions of salvaged bricks and roof tiles from the

Benjamin Franklin's "House" in Philadelphia, Pennsylvania, designed by Venturi, Scott Brown, and Associates in 1976. Photo undated. (Library of Congress, Prints & Photographs Division, photo by Carol M. Highsmith [LC-HS503-1061])

Palimpsest by Spencer Finch, installed at the Art Institute of Chicago, 2018. (Amy Hetletvedt)

province.[1] At the Memphis Slim Collaboratory, in Memphis, Tennessee (US), discussed in this chapter, the architects used salvaged material from the original home of blues musician Memphis Slim in a new structure that echoed the original house's form.

Physicality helps us remember. Author Orhan Pamuk constructed a novel about life in mid–twentieth-century Turkey around collected objects such as photographs, cigarette cartons, and toothbrushes and then created a museum in an Istanbul house to display them. Sometimes we remember by documenting, as Richard Nickel did, in the looming shadow of the wrecking ball. Or we solemnly curate the site of a horrible tragedy to mourn and honor those lost. Sometimes our hearts and community healing don't keep pace with nature's indefatigable regeneration, like red poppies waving over the fields of Flanders.

This chapter showcases four projects where artists, architects, and communities have activated an abandoned, vacant, or distressed structure in ways that can be interpreted poetically. The projects are titled to highlight the narrative role that the building assumes through the intervention. Whether on a building scale or a neighborhood scale, the poetic approach described in this chapter is not necessarily about preserving but rather initiating a dialogue about the forces and values shaping our communities. It's about giving voice to often-unacknowledged people or ways of life that have gone before. Author Emily P. Freeman says, "the gift of the artist doesn't only rest in the hands that sculpt but in the eyes that see. . . . And so we ought to pray not only for skill but for sight."[2] Like witness trees, whose scars identify their function in marking a threshold, some buildings can tell the stories of the things they've seen. Creative, poetic interventions into buildings in disinvested communities can help tell them.

"And so we ought to pray not only for skill but for sight."
—Emily P. Freeman

Conversations: The Heidelberg Project (Detroit, Michigan, US)

Whenever he encounters a particularly unusual object, my father-in-law exclaims, "Well, that's a conversation piece." It's an apt description of the Heidelberg Project in Detroit, widely considered one of the cornerstones of artistic interventions at the neighborhood scale.[3] Begun in 1986 by artist and Detroiter Tyree Guyton, the project transformed an entire block into an artistic statement and a hub for community activity.

As a teen, Guyton was encouraged by his grandfather to use a paintbrush rather than a weapon as a reaction to his discouragement about the state of his East Side Detroit neighborhood, which had faced depopulation and violence. Guyton began gathering cast-off items into sculptures and curated panoramas on empty lots and abandoned houses on Heidelberg Street, where his grandparents lived.

He used dolls, tires, bicycles, and clocks to create sculptures. He transformed houses by covering them with pennies or by painting them with the colorful dots that have become synonymous with the project. "I used what was available," Guyton says, "and so it was from the debris of the neighborhood that I created the Heidelberg Project landscape. There was no plan and no blueprint, just the will and determination to see beauty in the refuse."[4]

The home of Tyree Guyton's mother, on the corner of Chene and Canfield, 1998. (Walter P. Reuther Library, Archives of Labor and Urban Affairs, Wayne State University. Photo by Dale Rich. Dale Rich Collection. [rich_28048])

I read these colored dots as a commentary on the demolition process in the city. Although I can't find any documentation about this practice, my recollection from the early 2000s in Detroit is that houses identified for removal would receive spray-painted dots and letters on their façades, like hasty tattoos. "W" meant the water department had been through to cut off the water; "D" meant "demolish." Through his artistic intervention, Guyton paints an alternative label, a commentary about beauty, buildings, and what's been left behind.

The Heidelberg project has not been without controversy. As journalist John Gallagher points out, "No one was ever neutral about the Heidelberg project."[5] On one hand, Guyton was honored with city and state awards for his work, and the project achieved international renown. On the other, it has

Vacant houses in Brush Park, Detroit, with stenciled D, 2002. (Amy Hetletvedt)

House and car on Heidelberg Street, 1987. (Library of Congress, Prints & Photographs Division, Balthazar Korab Collection [LC-DIG-ppmsca-72262])

been the target of demolition, at least twelve arson fires since 2013,[6] and years of debate with the local McDougall-Hunt Citizens District Council. Although Guyton views his art as healing medicine, he's also called the project "a bitter pill to swallow."[7] It's not always easy to live in or near an unorthodox large-scale artistic installation, but according to executive director Jenenne Whitfield, the Heidelberg Project and the Citizens District Council eventually found commonalities and shared priorities in advocating for infrastructure improvements to the neighborhood.[8]

For its next chapter, the Heidelberg Project is moving toward a shared generation of art in its space.[9] The organization is prioritizing upgrades to the neighborhood, such as pedestrian and bike paths and visitor restrooms; creating community engagement spaces such as a gallery and rentable meeting space; and opening ways to integrate the work of new artists while preserving pieces of Guyton's and Heidelberg's legacy. Whitfield says, "The Heidelberg Project is not only wildly delightful and funky but also layered with complexities. It starkly represents the administration's ongoing failure to address existing neighborhoods in a meaningful way."[10] Or, as architecture professor Andrew Herscher phrased it in an examination of art production in the context of abandonment, "The city government's demolition program reflects its inability to manage decline."[11]

The Heidelberg Project, in Herscher's view, also "comprised a material address to an urban audience that otherwise would pay no attention to abandonment or accept it as a regrettable but unremarkable feature of Detroit's landscape."[12] Amid transformations, both external and internal to the Heidelberg project, Guyton's vision follows a continuing legacy of persistence, drawing Detroiters, visitors, artists, and administration into the conversation.

Interlocutors: The Marysburg Project and *The Dollhouse* (Marysburg, Saskatchewan, and Sinclair, Manitoba, Canada)

Heather Benning is a farmer and a large-scale sculptor in Saskatchewan, Canada. Her work centers on themes of life on the prairie and the transformation of rural culture. Traditionally rural areas in Canada have faced population loss related to urbanization that has depleted support for economic and civic activities.[13] Speaking of her upbringing and the phenomenon of families leaving farming in the 1990s, Benning says, "You can drive down any road and within a few miles you'll see another abandoned yard, and those skeletons left behind all have their own story."[14]

For *The Marysburg Project*, Benning selected an abandoned farmhouse in Saskatchewan as the container for an overscaled sculpture of a woman, which she fabricated on site in 2004. The woman is monochromatic, staring blankly across the horizon. Her head emerges from the roof and her hand from a window, reminding us of those whose hands, minds, and wearying

Part of the Heidelberg Project, 2019. (Library of Congress, Prints & Photographs Division, photo by Carol M. Highsmith [LC-DIG-highsm-60306])

work shaped both the physical and cultural landscape that we now know. Says Benning, "The labour of early prairie farmwomen was immense; they were consumed by their homes and land as their homes and land consumed them."[15]

Benning received positive feedback on the project from community members. "During its existence, I had several senior farm women thank me

Torso in the interior of *The Marysburg Project: Watching Woman*, 2004. (Photo by Heather Benning)

for creating the work. One woman in particular told me how she spent her life being Mrs. Joe (insert last name) and she was never known to the community by her name, and her contributions to the family farm. She had me over for dinner. She was a brilliant woman. Their farm was one of the first organic farms in the area."[16]

For a project in rural Manitoba, Benning selected another abandoned farmhouse, now adjacent to a busy highway in an area of flat rural prairie.

Exterior of *The Marysburg Project: Watching Woman*, 2004. (Photo by Heather Benning)

Over eighteen months, Benning replaced the roof, made some repairs and restorations, and then removed the back wall of the house and replaced it with plexiglass sheet. She furnished the interior to the period of its abandonment in 1968 and called it *The Dollhouse*. In a powerful reversal of minimalization, Benning maximized the dollhouse to full scale, which allowed it to become a setting for the current, everyday life of the community.

"Over the years of people driving around the house to view it, a roundabout driveway was formed," said Benning. "When I checked in on the house

The Dollhouse at dusk, 2007. (Photo by Heather Benning)

in 2010, there was evidence that someone had carefully let themselves into the house. There was a handwritten note saying they proposed to their girlfriend at the kitchen table, and she said yes. I was also told by locals that at shift change some of the oil men would stop at the house to have beer in the yard, if it was a nice day."[17]

In both *The Marysburg Project* and *The Dollhouse*, Benning reuses discarded structures and objects. By reframing them as large-scale sculptures

Reflection in *The Dollhouse*, 2007. (Photo by Heather Benning)

that, by virtue of their prairie surroundings, are visible for miles around, she brings a past to us, looming on the horizon. Past in present. An unavoidable encounter.

Like the work of artist Gordon Matta-Clark, who in the 1960s also used abandoned homes as media for social commentary, Benning's projects are often temporary. Matta-Clark's *Splitting* was demolished a few months after his radical intervention. The materials used to construct the sculpture (plaster) were not permanent in Benning's *The Marysburg Project*, which was destroyed by vandalism in 2011. *The Dollhouse* remained on the Manitoba landscape for six years and was destroyed by a controlled burn in 2013, which was documented on film. "This controlled burn was a part of the plan from the beginning," says Benning. "The film asks viewers to reckon with the unique grief caused by losing a home. This is particularly poignant at a time when we're increasing losing our home-places to unfettered industry and climate change."[18]

I have friends rebuilding their lives after losing their home to wildfire in Colorado. In early 2025 fires raged through Los Angeles. Another major insurer recently declared that they will stop insuring areas of Florida.[19] It seems inevitable that climate effects such as floods and fires will increasingly make inhabited places uninhabitable, creating new areas of abandonment.

Splitting 2 (documentation of the action *Splitting* made in 1974 in New Jersey, United States). 1974, printed 1977. Gelatin silver print. Sheet 8 × 11 1/16 in. (20.3 × 28.1 cm), image 7 5/8 × 11 11/16 in. (19.4 × 29.7 cm). (Gift of Harold Berg. Inv. N.: 2017.147. Artist: Matta-Clark, Gordon (1943–1978) © ARS, NY. Location: Whitney Museum of American Art/New York, NY/USA. © 2024 Estate of Gordon Matta-Clark/ Artists Rights Society (ARS), New York. Digital image © Whitney Museum of American Art/Licensed by Scala/Art Resource, NY)

Death of Dollhouse, 2013. (Photo by Heather Benning)

Some projects with narrative benefits, such as the Stony Island Arts Bank (profiled in Chapter 7), have a continuity in a neighborhood, but others, such as parts of the Heidelberg Project and *The Marysburg Project*, are ultimately dismantled and removed. Nevertheless, these projects should not be seen as a failure to conserve a building but as celebrations of their stories and as interlocutors, taking part in a dialogue about the climactic and societal forces that influence them.

The creative energy inserted into these structures has ennobled their endings, and by enlarging the scale of art to the scale of a home, a farmstead, and a neighborhood, these artistic approaches to existing buildings reaffirm the value of the lives led therein.

Witness for Justice: Ben Roy's Service Station (Money, Mississippi, US)

In the summer of 1955, fourteen-year-old African American Emmett Till was visiting his cousins in Money, Mississippi. On August 24, he entered Bryant's Grocery and interacted with the White proprietor, Carolyn Bryant, in some way, the details of which are not precisely known to the public.[20] Carolyn Bryant's husband, Roy Bryant, and J. W. Milam later abducted and brutally murdered Emmett Till, dumping his body in a river. Bryant and Milam were acquitted by jury.

Emmett Till's mother, Mamie Till-Mobley, chose an open casket for her son's funeral in Chicago. "Let the people see what they did to my boy," were her words.[21] Till's funeral and the images of Till in his casket, published by *Jet* magazine, are credited with galvanizing a generation of civil rights activists in the 1950s. No one who has seen these images can forget them. They stand as witness.

Although it changed hands, the grocery remained in business as a country store for three decades after Till's murder. In the mid-1980s, it was acquired by the Tribble family, who also own the Ben Roy's Service Station adjacent to the grocery.[22] Ray Tribble was one of the jurors in the 1955 trial of Bryant and Milam.

While the grocery fell into ruin, the wooden roadside service station was restored in 2013. This case study highlights not the restoration itself but the adjacency of the restored building to the ruin.

Long-closed and now vine-covered site of Bryant's Grocery in the crossroads community of Money, Mississippi. Ben Roy's Service Station is behind the grocery, 2016. (Library of Congress, Prints & Photographs Division, photo by Carol M. Highsmith [LC-DIG-highsm-42666])

Ben Roy's Service Station before restoration, circa 2012. (Courtesy of Beard + Riser Architects PLLC)

Ben Roy's Service Station after restoration, 2013. (Courtesy of Beard + Riser Architects PLLC)

Although the different outcomes of these two neighboring structures evoke many questions, as a technique, the restoration of an adjacent building to a site of memory or ruin is worth consideration for several reasons. First, the cost of restoring a ruin is likely to be greater than that of a more intact adjacent building. Second, the potential restoration of a ruin requires much more new material, leading to myriad interpretive questions such as which parts and periods should be reconstructed and how.

Finally, as Dave Tell, leader of the Emmett Till Memory Project, points out, the very existence of the ruin, the remains, becomes part of the story, and the adjacent restored building becomes a vantage point, physically and philosophically, for the ruin. Tell discusses the complicated relationship between these structures and their histories:

> In these twin histories of abandonment and preservation, we see how race, place, and commemoration shift together. As soon as the Bryants' store was allowed to crumble, the forensic fascination of who-did-what-to-whom was reframed as an examination of how racism persists in the Delta. The onset of ruin has transformed the focus of commemorative inquiry: the inattention of the local community is now part of the meaning of Till's murder. And while the haunted ruins of Bryant's Grocery suggest that the Delta has not adequately dealt with the murder of Emmett Till, the countermemorial at Ben Roy's argues that there was not much to deal with in the first place. Over and over again, we see that the Mississippi Delta is not simply the place where Till was killed or the setting where memory work happens. It is an ingredient part of the work itself.[23]

The Emmett Till Interpretive Center, located in a storefront in Sumner, Mississippi, about 30 miles away from Ben Roy's Service Station and Bryant's Grocery, also has a narrative vantage point. It is situated directly across from the Tallahatchie County Courthouse, where the trial took place. The sites in Sumner; the river landing in Glendora, Mississippi, where Till's body was found; and the church on Chicago's South Side where his funeral was held were established as a multisite national monument in 2023.

Among a network of sites, Ben Roy's Service Station stands as witness to what happened next door, a witness to how we choose to remember and what we keep. It asks us to see.

A view of Bryant's Grocery, 2016. (Library of Congress, Prints & Photographs Division, photo by Carol M. Highsmith [LC-DIG-highsm-42662])

Witness for Peace: Bombed Out Church (Liverpool, Merseyside, UK)

On May 6, 1941, shortly after midnight, an incendiary device hit St. Luke's church in Liverpool as part of the German Luftwaffe's May Blitz, igniting a fire that burned for three days. The fire consumed the roof and most of the interior, leaving only a smoldering shell. Constructed in the early nineteenth century in the perpendicular gothic style, the church's bell tower contained what is believed to be the earliest known cast iron bell frame, which survived the fire.[24]

St. Luke's Church, Leece Street, Liverpool. A view from beneath the chancel arch looking west toward the tower in the bombed-out ruins, 1963. (© Crown Copyright. Historic England Archive)

The remaining structure was closed to the public for decades after the Blitz. A growing contingent of people believed that the site should be left as a ruin to memorialize the bombing and those who lost their lives in the war.

In 2007, the nonprofit group Urban Strawberry Lunch opened the church to the public for the first time since the bombing. Now simply called Bombed Out Church, the site is operated as a managed ruin and venue for multidisciplinary arts and community events. These temporary uses have included theater, musical events, cinema, and art installations. The site also hosts remembrance and educational events. For one event, local school children fabricated poppies from recycled bottles and placed them around the sculpture called *Truce* at the site.

Around the world, there are other examples of managed World War II ruins as memorials. The entire French village of Oradour-sur-Glane is a memorial, remaining exactly as it was in June 1944, rusting cars parked on the streets. Genbaku Dome is preserved as a partial ruin, the only structure left standing in the area of the atomic bomb blast in Hiroshima, Japan.[25] Man-

Truce, a memorial sculpture by Andy Edwards at the garden of St. Luke's Church in Liverpool. Photo 2022. (Ed Rooney/Alamy Stock Photo)

aged ruins usually involve interpretive features and spaces for passage, reflection, and assembly through the site.

Although these sites were destroyed by war, a managed ruin can be an approach to a structure in a disinvested community. For example, the now disused Vítkovice factory in the Czech Republic, whose pathways are mentioned in Chapter 6, has become a venue for various community activities, pop-ups, and an interpretive site about its past industrial history.

At St. Luke's, digital technologies have been used to document its stories, connecting the present to the past. An oral history project called "Finest Hour Sound Archive" trained youth to interview Blitz witnesses and capture their stories on audio. Most people are familiar with the British wartime propaganda poster "Keep Calm and Carry On." Other concurrent posters with slogans such as "Make Do and Mend" and "Save Scrap for Victory" express the collective wartime ethos that carries into the philosophy undergirding this particular site of memory today. In the words of the Bombed

This window at St. Luke's Church contains the cracked remains of the Greek letter omega (the last letter of the Greek alphabet), used to signify the end. For this church building, it is not yet the end. Photo 2018. (Rodhullandemu, CC BY-SA 4.0 <https://creativecommons.org/licenses/by-sa/4.0>, via Wikimedia Commons)

People skate on an ice rink installed inside St. Luke's Church in Liverpool, 2023. (PA Images/Alamy Stock Photo)

Out Church organization, the building stands as a "testament to community spirit."[26] Resilience amid damage, continuance despite damage, remembering and renewing at the same time.

Memory Markers: Collected Thoughts and Examples

Many of us have returned to a place that was important to us as children to find the scale much different from what we remembered. Most of us have left behind places that are impossible to revisit. How does memory reconstruct these significant places? Which features are persistent? Which become larger? Which are brought with us in the travel cases of our minds?

In 2017, MIT's Future Heritage Lab documented resident-initiated design projects at the Azraq refugee camp in Jordan, which were collected in an exhibit called *Design to Live: Everyday Inventions from a Refugee Camp*.[27] One

Theaster Gates's sculpture explores the themes of migration, portability, and memory. (Theaster Gates, *Migration Rickshaw for Sleeping, Building and Playing*, 2013. Wood, fabric, Huguenot House wallpaper and wheel, 57 × 127 × 27 3/16 in. (144.8 × 322.6 × 69 cm). © Theaster Gates. Photo © White Cube [Edouard Fraipont])

of the projects in this exhibit was called "Desert Castle," in which residents reconstructed pieces of the citadel of Aleppo as an act of cultural preservation, reconstructing it not as it was but as they remembered it with the materials that they had available. Archaeological accuracy is not primary in this reconstruction, but associative memory is. The reconstruction can be seen as a social sculpture, an occupant-led initiative built on a shared memory.

Displaced communities experience the loss of cultural resources through separation. Disinvested communities experience the loss of cultural resources through demolition, extraction, and the slow processes of decay. Both disinvested communities and displaced communities can remember by rebuilding structures that have been destroyed or reconstructing sites from which they've been painfully disconnected.

Carlos Nielbock is a sculptor and metalworker who grew up in Germany. His mother was German and his father a World War II soldier from Detroit. As described by Sarah Rose Sharp in an article for *ModelD*, "His early experiences as a person of mixed race in post-war Celle, Germany, included his intensive training as a skilled metalsmith under the tutelage of monks in Celle, and a sense of alienation that in part caused him to seek out his father in Detroit."[28]

Dismantling the statues on the tower during the Detroit City Hall demolition, 1961. (Walter P. Reuther Library, Archives of Labor and Urban Affairs, Wayne State University. Detroit News Collection. [vmc_70789-1])

Pieces of the clock and statuary from the Detroit City Hall demolition, 1961. (Walter P. Reuther Library, Archives of Labor and Urban Affairs, Wayne State University. Detroit News Collection. [vmc_70789])

After finding his Detroit family, Sharp describes, Nielbock "leveraged his craftsman training to make a start for himself in the business of reconstructing the architectural, ornamental metalwork that is the fading legacy of Detroit's more affluent days."[29] Nielbock has proposed a project to reconstruct the clock tower from Detroit's City Hall whose demolition was described in Chapter 4. He envisions a multisensory recreation using the statues of the four virtues that adorned the tower as an "interactive community public art piece,"[30] celebrating the spirit of technical innovation that fueled the city.

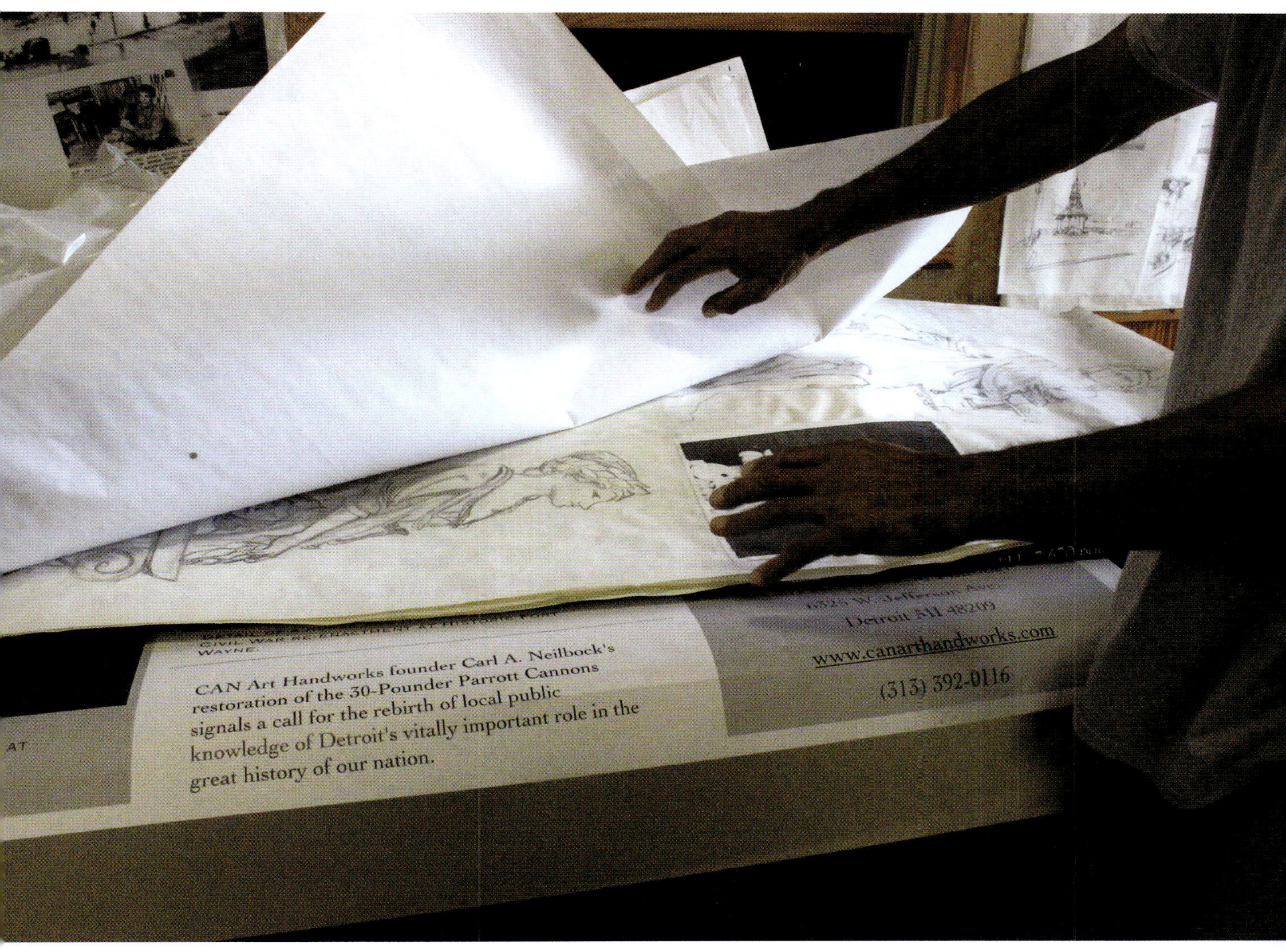

Neilbock discusses his design ideas for the clock tower, 2016. (Photo by Sarah Rose Sharp)

I am fascinated by how Nielbock's own skills and imagination, along with those of others who will work on the project, could combine these artifacts with new materials. I'm curious about how the demolition of that City Hall, which artist William Allison Bostick called a "public execution,"[31] could become a public resurrection. Rather than restoring in a technical sense, could an interpretive reconstruction change or challenge Detroit's narratives?

Panorama of neighborhood, Memphis Slim house at left, circa 2013. (Courtesy of brg3s)

In Memphis, Tennessee (US), the nonprofit Community LIFT and numerous partners organized around the idea of creating a collaborative music center at the home of John Len Chatman, later known as Memphis Slim, who developed his blues style while jamming on the front porch of the Memphis home with other legendary local musicians. Sometime around 2010, the vacant house sustained extensive damage from a fallen tree and remained open to the elements. When a team from brg3s architects surveyed the house in 2014, they found that it was also sitting on compromised foundations. As discussed in Chapter 1, a preservation emphasis on the integrity of the structure can funnel efforts toward structures that are well maintained, unchanged, or undeteriorated.

How to preserve the spirit of the house and its spatial role in the history of blues music? In the case of the Memphis Slim house, the architects developed an interpretive proposal for what would become the Memphis Slim Collaboratory. The new structure's street façade echoes the original form and proportions of the house, and some interior elements, such as the primary stairway, maintain their original location. Reclaimed wood was used for the framing, and reclaimed bricks reconstructed the fireplace in the new music culture

Memphis Slim house front, circa 2013.
(Photo by Ken West)

Memphis Slim Collaboratory, 2014.
(Photo by Ken West)

center. The reclamation and interpretation of the original house honors the resourcefulness and creativity of Memphis Slim, who transformed his life experiences into an upbeat musical energy.

Memory or interpretive reconstructions use available materials to tell a narrative. The narrative is not only about the structure itself but about how a person interprets the structure, like a musical riff in the blues, or how a

Porch jam at the Collaboratory during the Soulsville USA Festival, 2014. (Photo by Ken West)

community remembers a place, like a collaborated musical jam that is somehow more than the sum of its parts. Interpretive reconstruction projects reflect the distortion of remembrance, stretching out like the melted watches in Dalí's *The Persistence of Memory*, into the space between the place and our precious, present recollection.

Memphis Slim Collaboratory interior, 2014. (Photo by Ken West)

Builders No. 2 was painted during a time of social and racial upheaval in the United States. Despite its jagged geometry and the menacing visual of the saw blades and drill bits, the painting has a hopeful, almost reverent quality: bright colors, floating tools readily at hand, three people working in triangular harmony, like a trinity. (*Builders No. 2*, 1968. Gouache and tempera on paper. 30 × 21 1/4 in. [76.2 × 54 cm]. Artist: Jacob Lawrence [1917–2000] © ARS, NY. Location: Reynolds House Museum of American Art/Winston-Salem, NC/USA. © 2024 The Jacob and Gwendolyn Knight Lawrence Foundation, Seattle/Artists Rights Society [ARS], New York. Photo: The Jacob and Gwendolyn Lawrence Foundation/Art Resource, NY)

Chapter 6

The Prosaic: Activating Buildings Through Practical Interventions

"He looked awful. But he said very patiently and very carefully, 'Johnny, I would be honored if anything I gave you could actually be used for something important—if it were to have any special purpose, I'd be very proud.' That was when I first began to think about certain events or specific things being 'important' and having 'special purpose.'"

—John Irving, *A Prayer for Owen Meany*

In the challenging context of disinvestment, can buildings in a community have a special purpose? Can the broken environment become a useful tool for regeneration?

The use value of structures plays a crucial role in disinvested communities because it taps into their regenerative capacity. Rather than viewing a vacant or distressed property as a resource consumer, it can be helpful to reframe the property as a resource provider. How can the building or structure fill a need? What does it have to offer? Could its special purpose be a usefulness in the present tense? Can a property's resources be matched with needs?

During periods of high vacancy in a community, there are creative opportunities for symbiotic benefits of temporary tenants in vacant buildings. Vacant properties could become supportive physical and social structures to help vulnerable populations transition into more permanent situations. A 2014 study in Europe estimated that there was enough vacant housing for twice the number of all people experiencing homelessness on the continent.[1] Ireland recently organized a program for owners to offer vacant housing to Ukrainian refugees.[2] Around the world, heritage organizations are beginning to study opportunities for adapting historic buildings for refugees.[3]

In Seattle, Washington (US), a nonprofit called WELD Seattle connects people transitioning from incarceration to a local community, including support for employment and housing. One of their programs, called Empty to Essential, encourages property holders and real estate developers with vacant property to temporarily donate it to WELD for use as transitional, recovery housing. While WELD members live there, they maintain the properties and pay utilities, creating a mutually beneficial relationship between property owners and people reentering the community.

Says WELD development director Erica Wiley, "Seattle is a very difficult real estate market with a dearth of affordable housing. This program offers a temporary solution to keep empty properties earning, while providing a safe spot to land for people at a critical point of re-integration."[4] Sherri, a mail carrier in Seattle, shared this about a property occupied by WELD tenants: "I have had this route for over 10 years, and so I've seen this vacant property in a whole variety of states. These guys do a real good job maintaining the property, and they're always respectful and kind."[5]

Economic crises such as the Great Depression and more recently the Great Recession (2008–2009), environmental crises such as the Dust Bowl, and natural disasters such as hurricanes and earthquakes disrupt values and spur migration. Cities such as Detroit experience cycles of growth and abandonment, migration in and migration out. We lived in our Detroit home for ten years. Jane, who lived there before us, lived there sixty. But the truth is that in the long run we're all temporary tenants. The only difference is the length of our stay.

Possibilities can emerge when communities view underused structures with a shorter occupancy time frame in mind. Not sixty years, nor six years, but maybe sixty days? Or six? Experiments with temporary occupancy have documented positive changes in how communities view the vacant spaces and how temporary occupancy aids in envisioning more flexible solutions, thus creating value.[6] The knowledge base is growing about how professionals and regulating bodies can facilitate various lengths of occupancy safely and legally. Furthermore, as architect and urban designer Matteo Robiglio points out, temporary uses bolster hope, "providing residents tangible signs that regeneration processes will not leave them behind."[7]

In 2003, I walked through an abandoned six-story apartment building in Detroit with a client. The grand brick building, called the St. Rita, had last been occupied sometime in the 1990s as subsidized housing. In 2003, it still retained many of its original architectural features, including my personal favorite, the built-in Murphy beds that swung out from intricate wood-paneled walls.

When my client and I walked through again in 2006, as her organization persisted in its attempts to fund a rehabilitation for the building, much more of the original detail was missing. As time went on, the building's future became more precarious: The property ownership and title were stuck in a morass of uncertainty as the St. Rita was sold at foreclosure auction, back taxes built up, and the building spent time on the city's emergency demolition list.

The St. Rita was rehabilitated by a different architect–client–developer team as supportive housing for veterans in 2019. It was a win for the building and a win for the community. But had the building been able to secure a temporary tenant during the many years that it remained vacant, it could have brought life to the building and nearby blocks and would probably have been able to retain more of the original architectural detailing.

Temporary uses for vacant buildings are sometimes called "meanwhile" uses. Nicolas Bosetti, a researcher manager for the Centre for London, says, "One of the main barriers to meanwhile use is the perception that hoarding a site is safer. Often the opposite is true. Opening a site to a community and encouraging interaction with residents usually sees a reduction in antisocial activity."[8]

"Curtsey while you're thinking what to say. It saves time."
—Lewis Carroll

A British organization called Meanwhile Space is a social enterprise that advocates for bringing temporarily unused space and vacant assets back into use. A project overview from Meanwhile[9] quoted Lewis Carroll's character, The Red Queen, to capture the essence of the meanwhile approach: "Curtsey while you're thinking what to say. It saves time."[10] A prosaic or practical use for an underused building can be a curtsy while longer-range plans are considered and developed. It can also be a prototype for future uses.

St. Rita lobby with marble column intact, 2003. (Amy Hetletvedt)

A large site transformation in Paris offers multiple lessons in how opening a site can test out new uses for old buildings and stitch an underused place back into the heart of the city. The St. Vincent de Paul Hospital served mothers and infants in Paris's 14th Arrondissement for over a century. In the early 2000s the hospital was phased out of service. After the hospital's closure in 2011, the Parisian city government began considering plans to redevelop the 3.2-hectare site into an ecodistrict. But the question remained: What to do with the large vacant urban site in the meantime?

Through a proposal process, the groups Aurore Association, YesWeCamp, and Plateau Urbain were given the authority to use and manage the site for five intermediate years. They planned to use the site to contribute to the common good through a variety of programs and initiatives that would demonstrate the value of maintaining some of the temporary initiatives in the long-term plan. Their program was called *Les Grands Voisins*, great neighbors.

Les Grands Voisins used the buildings and the open spaces between them to accommodate pop-up restaurants and bars, emergency shelter, artist spaces, cultural activities, and even camping sites. In the five years that the

St. Rita lobby with marble column felled and the marble wall panel adjacent to the lower door missing, 2006. (Amy Hetletvedt)

project ran, it housed 1,000 people, employed 2,000 people, and hosted 300 events, and the day center for refugees and technical assistance was visited by 46,000 people.[11] A "Solidarity Concierge Service" interfaced between local residents around the site, the visiting public, people experiencing situations of need or social exclusion, and all the stakeholders at the Voisins.

Opening weekend at Les Grands Voisins, 2015. (Yann Guillotin)

Welcome center for the Les Grands Voisins camping area, 2015. (Lisa George, Yes We Camp)

Les Grands Voisins focused on sustainability, reducing waste, and helping each other. For example, refrigerators located throughout the site allowed dining establishments and food vendors to deposit surplus food, where hungry people could retrieve it for free.[12] A recycle shop and resource center was a place for people to donate and shop for household goods and to attend classes on repair and creative reuse. The beneficial use of the lower floors of several buildings by businesses "operating in the social and inclusive economy" and creative enterprises was "confirmed by the transitional occupancy of Les Grands Voisins."[13]

The activities at Les Grands Voisins influenced the future not only of the St. Vincent de Paul site but of temporary use throughout Paris. According to a Paris Metropolitan government publication about the project, "The success of the experience revealed the benefit of combining programmes—emergency shelter, crafts, creation, food, culture, discussion."[14] In 2019, the City of Paris signed a Charter for the Development of Temporary Occupation as a Tool Serving the Parisian Territory. The charter, which recognizes the benefits of temporary occupation for a more flexible, sustainable, and inclusive city, was signed at Les Grands Voisins.

Chickens as part of the Les Grands Voisins urban agriculture project, 2016. (Lisa George Yes We Camp)

Carnival at Les Grands Voisins, 2020. (Sara Simula)

Les Grands Voisins closed officially in 2020. The mix of activities at the site covered its costs during the period that it operated and kept the district alive with activity. In the new ecodistrict on the site, which is being developed at the writing of this book, 60 percent of the buildings will be preserved and combined with new buildings and open spaces.[15] In a way that would make St. Vincent de Paul smile, the former hospital site demonstrated a marvelous capacity to give and to heal.

The projects featured in this chapter demonstrate how welcoming tourists, gig workers, people experiencing homelessness, and even agriculture to an unoccupied site can provide benefits to those whom the building hosts and to the neighborhood. For example, The Million Donkey Hotel offered an authentic travel experience to the adventurous traveler, benefiting the economy of its village. De Ceuvel hosts nonprofits and social service organizations in repurposed vessels on a site that will eventually be repurposed. Most of the projects profiled in this chapter have transitioned or will transition into another use. Their temporary use provides benefits while testing out, in real time and space, which occupancy strategies gain momentum.

When proposing temporary or incremental uses for a building, there are legal hurdles, and often some upgrades must be undertaken to meet safety requirements. But experiments in municipal processes have yielded innovation here, too. Architect Michael Bohn describes a "self-certification" plan check, where in the state of California, a plan review can be eliminated when a registered professional certifies compliance. This helped a project in an unused industrial structure in the Los Angeles metro area move "from ideation to completion and move-in in only five months; as a direct result, the homeless population in the city of Bellflower declined by nearly 90%."[16]

This chapter showcases five projects where structures that are abandoned or in disrepair have creatively and incrementally been activated. The projects are titled to highlight their intermediate use or practical (prosaic) benefit. Work on the projects has been collaborative: partnerships between the community and architects, artists and nonprofits, municipalities and government agencies. At Bánffy Castle in Romania, groups of people repair the structure over time. In Pittsburgh, Pennsylvania (US), a nonprofit and a community group teamed up to tackle the complex and costly portions of renovating the exterior of the Denny Row Houses, leaving space for the residents to personalize and fit out interior renovations over time. A similar strategy was used in the housing that Elemental designed in Chile and the ModPod in the Project Row Houses community in the United States, which is discussed in Chapter 10.

Creativity invites creativity and participation, conserving the past and building social collateral. In neighborhoods and communities where resources are scarce and the scale of a building's needs seems large or overwhelming, pursuing short-term, partial, or incremental practical uses for a site offers a beneficial way forward.

Shelter: Million Donkey Hotel (Prata Sannita, Italy)

Older structures and community viability in many European small towns are at risk as residents are increasingly drawn to seek work in urban centers. In Italy, more than 5,000 *borghi* (villages) are at risk of depopulation, and 2,000 are at risk of abandonment.[17] In the remote Italian village of Prata Sannita, with a population of about 1,500, population migration has left numerous abandoned buildings, particularly in the medieval part of the village (Pratta Inferiore), where most of the population is elderly.

A group of architects based in Austria called feld72 was invited to the Italian village as part of the "Village of Art" project focused on identity and social space within territories, commissioned by Paesesaggio Workgroup, Region Campania, and financed by the European Union. Addressing the need to revitalize both the spaces in the village and the local economy, the architects suggested an innovative solution that would cater to the modern traveler: "to view Prata Sannita as a large, scattered hotel that has rooms available in the abandoned buildings."[18]

A platform bed in one of the Prata Sannita hotel rooms overlooks the village, 2006. (© Hertha Hurnaus)

Individual guest rooms and a public bathroom were installed in abandoned spaces throughout the medieval town. Using simple, readily available materials, the project was completed within one month, and the cost was less than 10,000 euros, thanks in part to more than forty residents who donated their time and labor toward the project and subsequently managed the hotel.

The renovated spaces were sources of revenue during the tourist season and served as community gathering spaces during the off-season. The project is called the Million Donkey Hotel in honor of all the people who provided

A community work day on the Million Donkey Hotel, 2006. (feld72)

labor to help realize this project on a hillside. According to feld72 partner Anne Catherine Fleith, the hotel name emerged as a response to a comment from a journalist, who said, "You would need one million donkeys to realize this idea!"[19] In the words of feld72, the Million Donkey Hotel demonstrates "vacancy activation through participation."[20]

As each abandoned space becomes linked with other spaces, a network is formed. The social network of residents who cooperatively renovated and run the hotel is interwoven with this spatial network. The community is strengthened, and the narrative takes a new turn: Emptiness has become an opportunity for hospitality.

A community work day on the Million Donkey Hotel, 2006. (feld72)

A stairway and handrail installed for the Million Donkey Hotel project, 2006. (© Hertha Hurnaus)

The scattered site model allows smaller structures and spaces to be connected as one operational entity. Another example of the scattered site model is The Inn at Ferry Street in Detroit, which is a collection of single-family homes along one block in Midtown Detroit that were rehabilitated and organized as forty hotel suites in 2001.[21] It's a larger investment and a more

The bathroom installed as part of the Million Donkey Hotel project, 2006. (© Hertha Hurnaus)

detailed finish level than Million Donkey's spare, minimalist style. Yet it has been an anchor to the academic–institutional Midtown area of Detroit for twenty years. Both scattered site projects, the Million Donkey Hotel and the Inn at Ferry Street, demonstrate how creative, community-oriented solutions can meet multiple needs (in this case, the needs of travelers and needs of locals), thus increasing the impact.

The Inn on Ferry Street, Detroit, 2024. (Amy Hetle-vedt)

Gardens: Plant Concert in the City Club (Newburgh, New York, US)

Redeveloping vacant lots into parks and gardens is a cornerstone of revitalization efforts in many disinvested communities. Urban agriculture gardens become gathering places and are a way to build community and provide nutritious food via raised beds.

Vacant buildings also present opportunities for urban agriculture. The Michigan Urban Farming Initiative, for example, piloted a rainwater-harvesting cistern in Detroit in 2017 in the basement of a deconstructed house.[22] In a case study on adaptive building reuse for urban vertical agriculture, Elizabeth Yarina, a designer and planner working in the areas of sustainability and resilience said, "In shrinking post-industrial cities, large swathes of buildings have been abandoned that lend themselves to new uses as vertical urban farms. In denser and growing cities, appropriating buildings that are structurally sound but no longer useful for their intended purpose, or rooftops and balconies on functioning buildings, can provide hyper-local food using a minimum of space."[23]

In vacant buildings that remain intact (in other words, buildings that still have roofs), agriculture must be supported by lighting and irrigation. These can be provided with industrial rack-type systems. Structures that are already roofless are opportunities for gardens because of available sunlight and exposure to weather.

In Newburgh, New York, a town on the Hudson River Valley about 60 miles outside of New York City, an artistic installation in 2021 provided a vision of this potential for a historic building. The City Club, a two-story brick and brownstone building, was constructed between 1852 and 1857. Originally a residence, it was one of the first collaborations of Andrew Jackson Downing and Calvert Vaux. Downing and Vaux were prolific producers of residential house and garden plans in the late nineteenth century. Downing was also a landscape designer, working on gardens for the Smithsonian and the White House. Vaux went on to work on designs for Central Park with Frederick Law Olmsted.

The residence that Downing and Vaux designed in Newburgh, which was also the hometown of Downing, was purchased by a men's social club in 1901. Beginning in the 1960s, the upper floors housed a local law library. A profile on Newburgh in *The Guardian* details the plight of the city in the latter half of the twentieth century and provides context for the history of the City Club: "Once one of the grandest cities in the entire north-east, the story of Newburgh's decline and the fight to resurrect it is the story of the struggle of many cities in the United States, a story that says much about how the nation views its urban centres, and the problems and challenges that go with them."[24]

In 1970, the Newburgh Urban Renewal Agency demolished the vacant hotel adjacent to the City Club, and the club building's potential removal was the subject of debate. By 1976, the dust temporarily settled on the demolition debate as restorationist Brian Thompson purchased the City Club building and construction was completed on a new library and plaza next door.

The City Club, originally the Dr. William A. M. Culbert House (120 Grand Street, Newburgh, New York), photographed in 1970. (Library of Congress, Prints & Photographs Division, HABS, reproduction number HABS NY,36-NEWB,11—3)

However, the reprieve was short. Only five years later (in 1981), the City Club building was gutted by fire and has been abandoned since. Although the roof was lost in the fire, steel beams, which had been added in 1909,[25] stabilized the structure. Despite the building's prominence by location and as one of the remaining Downing–Vaux collaborations in Downing's hometown, the building remained unoccupied and underused and has continued to decay in the four decades since the fire.

Aerial of the City Club building, 2021. (Photo by James Holland, Courtesy Strongroom, Inc.)

In 2017, conceptual artist Martin Roth, known for his explorations of art involving living organisms, was invited by Strongroom, an organization dedicated to presenting site-specific contemporary art installations, to consider a project in Newburgh. Upon visiting Newburgh and seeing trees growing out of the City Club building, Roth envisioned transforming the space with plants and biofeedback mechanisms to create sound.

When Roth passed away in 2019 before realizing the project, Strongroom continued Roth's initiative. Strongroom worked with the City of Newburgh (the current City Club building owner), which required a third-party engineer to sign off on the building safety aspects of the project. An engineer assessed the site and developed a list of stipulations for the temporary occupancy—for example, blocking certain sidewalks and vacating the structure in case of wind or rain. Years of background work culminated in the 2021 plant concert installation and events.

Roth's concept emphasized how human presence in the building would change the sound in the garden. This harks back to concepts of original gardens such as Eden, the delicate balance of human and nature, the partnership of cultivation, and Downing and Vaux's visions for gardens in the city.

I view Roth's concept and Strongroom's installation as a shift of Downing's picturesque ideals. Instead of romantic, can a garden be regenerative? Instead

Doors are open a- the City Club during the Plant Concert, a verdant invitation, 2021. (Photo by James Holland, courtesy Strongroom, Inc.)

of a passive setting, can it be an active strategy, a participant in regeneration? Considering dichotomies in the perceptions of ruins discussed in Chapter 1, I return to Sidney Robinson's quote, "Not having the money or the time to correct the depredations of gravity, water, growth and decay is one thing. To cultivate them is another."[26] Interventions with ruins can use this question as

The interior of the City Club during the plant concert, with the stabilizing steel beams, 2021. (Photo by James Holland, courtesy Strongroom, Inc.)

a sort of examen (the spiritual practice of reflection) and a sounding board with the community. What will a proposed intervention cultivate? Further decay or future growth?

As for the City Club, the City of Newburgh is looking into plans for redevelopment as of the writing of this book. In one sense, Strongroom was limited in what they could do with and for the building because they did not have ownership. But their limits also underlined the essential transience of the built environment. Strongroom executive director Kelly Schroer relays an anecdote about Peter Del Tredici, a local botanist who noticed a young tulip tree inside the City Club while giving tours of the urban plants. Del Tredici later discovered a mature tulip tree a block or so away that could have been planted by Downing given its size and age. "So," concludes Schroer, "perhaps a progeny of a tree planted by Downing himself is growing in the City Club. It made me think that this building and its maker made their own story that continues to this day, with or without our interventions."[27]

Another interior view during the plant concert. 2021. (Photo by James Holland, courtesy Strongroom. Inc.)

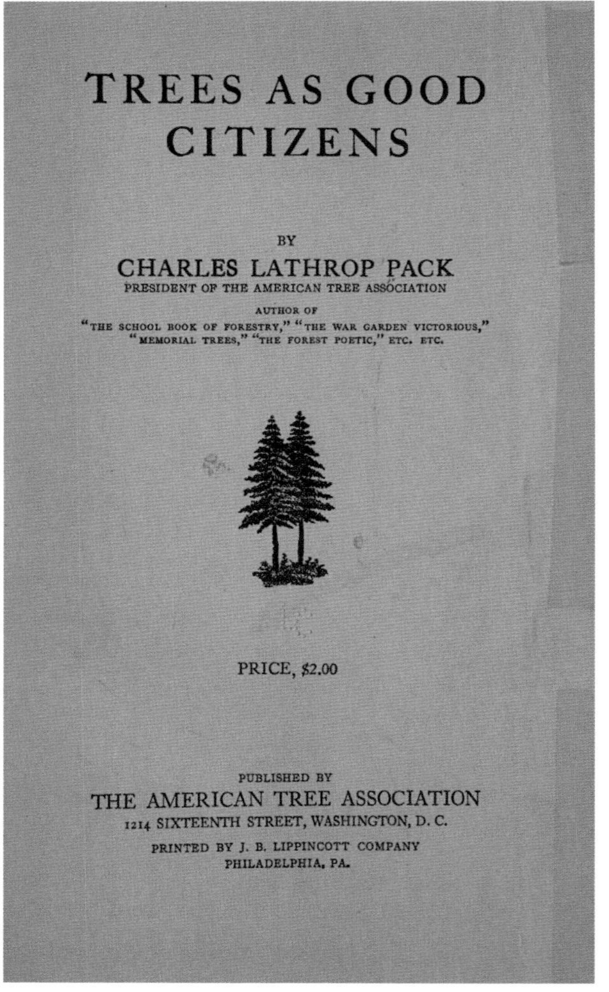

TREES AS GOOD CITIZENS

BY

CHARLES LATHROP PACK

PRESIDENT OF THE AMERICAN TREE ASSOCIATION

AUTHOR OF

"THE SCHOOL BOOK OF FORESTRY," "THE WAR GARDEN VICTORIOUS," "MEMORIAL TREES," "THE FOREST POETIC," ETC. ETC.

PRICE, $2.00

PUBLISHED BY

THE AMERICAN TREE ASSOCIATION

1214 SIXTEENTH STREET, WASHINGTON, D. C.

PRINTED BY J. B. LIPPINCOTT COMPANY

PHILADELPHIA, PA.

Title page from the book *Trees as Good Citizens* by Charles Lathrop Pack, 1922. Can trees, gardens, and landscape be participants in regeneration? (Public domain, Library of Congress, https://www.loc.gov/item/23001194/)

Across the country in Phoenix, Arizona, the sanctuary of a 1929 church that has been vacant and roofless since a fire in 1984 was stabilized and reimagined in 2024 as a nature-filled courtyard called the Monroe Street Abbey.[28] City Club's connection with Downing and the history of garden design is poetic. But the potential applications of the concept such as Roth's plant garden and the Monroe Street Abbey are also practical. When a building is in transition or a complete renovation or restoration is not achievable or desirable, cultivated plants—in combination with necessary structural or safety upgrades—can be occupants. A garden, whether for food or for beauty, can yield a harvest to benefit the community.

Remediation: De Ceuvel (Amsterdam, The Netherlands)

In 2012, the municipality of Amsterdam put out a request for bids (called a tender) for a former shipyard site on the Johan van Hasselt canal. It was a brownfield site, with environmental contamination from years of industrial activity. The city sought proposals for an intermediate use while a longer-range redevelopment plan was in progress.

A group of creatives including Smeele Architectures, Space&Matter Architects, and Delva Landscape Architects won a ten-year lease on the property with their proposal for De Ceuvel, and the lease has been recently extended.[29] Their overarching concept for the development: a living experiment for sustainable technology and practices, both ecological and social.

Instead of building new structures on the site, the group brought in derelict houseboats from around the city. The boats were adapted to provide space for nonprofits, startups, cafés, and social service organizations that energize the site with year-round activity. They were renovated with found materials and ecotechnologies.

A houseboat is craned into place on the De Ceuvel site, circa 2012. (Photo by Jean-Pierre Jans. Courtesy of Space&Matter)

De Ceuvel as seen from above, circa 2014. (Courtesy of Space&Matter)

The houseboats are connected by a wooden jetty that winds through the site, floating above the ground, which has been carefully planted with vegetation that will slowly clean and renew the soil. The technique, called phytoremediation, uses plants to stabilize and draw contaminants from the soil. The raised walkway facilitates temporary occupancy of the site, separating the human circulation between the boats from the cleaning work of the plants on the vegetation plane below.

Environmental contamination is a widespread societal problem that disproportionately affects lower-income communities. The United Church of Christ's 1987 report "Toxic Wastes and Race in the United States" cited race as the most important predictor of proximity to hazardous waste facilities in the United States.[30] Dorceta Taylor's 2014 book *Toxic Communities* expands on the field of environmental justice, coalescing scholarship on how hazardous and toxic sites' location and remediation coincide with race, income, mobility, and activism.[31] Research not only on the how and why but on what to do about brownfield sites is expanding.

Floating walkways connect the houseboats, De Ceuvel, circa 2014. (Photo by Martijn van Wijk. Courtesy of Space&Matter)

An evening musical event at De Ceuvel, circa 2014. (Courtesy of Space&Matter)

De Ceuvel's soil remediation builds on this growing scientific body, but the project also builds on artistic precedents, such as the work of artist Mel Chin. For an installation called *Safe House* (2008–2010) in New Orleans, Louisiana (US), Chin installed an oversized vault door on a vacant home and papered the interior with "Fundred" bills. The Fundreds, facsimiles of hundred-dollar bills interpreted and colored by children, were part of Chin's campaign Fundred, which lobbies for legislation to better protect children from lead poisoning, and OperationPayDirt, which studies and encourages remediation methods for lead contamination.

One of Chin's earlier works, *Revival Field* (1991), is an environmental sculpture to clean the soil at a hazardous waste landfill in St. Paul, Minnesota (US). "The new sculpture is plants," said Chin, discussing the project. "We live in a world of pollution with heavy metals saturating the soil, where there

SafeHouse New Orleans, circa 2008–2010. (Photo courtesy of the artist, Mel Chin)

is no solution to that. If that could be carved away, and life could return to that soil and then a diverse and ecologically balanced life, then that is a wonderful sculpture."[32]

At De Ceuvel, disused objects, the houseboats, come to the site as hosts for human activity, floating above the plane of remediation. It's worth noting that the houseboats repurposed in De Ceuvel are inherently mobile objects. Relocating architectural assets that were not designed to be mobile, whether through salvage or moving entire structures, brings with it sociological and ethical questions, some of which are discussed in Chapter 4.

At other disused industrial sites, separate circulation pathways are added. At the former Vítkovice steel plant in Ostrava, Czech Republic, elevated pathways lead through various levels of the decommissioned structure. Some of the spaces, like De Ceuvel, are used for music festivals and temporary exhibits.

Similar to the raised pathways at De Ceuvel, yellow handrails denote the tour pathways through the former Vítkovice factory in Ostrava, Czech Republic, 2020. (Amy Hetletvedt)

De Ceuvel's innovative approach is a remarkable example of temporary tenants. It is somewhat like having houseguests who host a fabulous party and then do all the dishes and clean the house before they leave. It demonstrates the value of the circular economy for temporary occupancy: repurposing houseboats that would have otherwise been discarded, providing space for collaborating, creativity, and social good, all while decontaminating the site. Bettering while between.

Education: Bánffy Castle (Bonţida, Romania)

The Bánffy Castle in Romania is a manor house that was fortified in the second half of the seventeenth century and expanded and modified throughout the centuries that followed. The castle complex, including its extensive stables, exhibits aesthetic features and spatial arrangements characteristic of various periods: Renaissance, Baroque, Classical, Rococo, and Neo-Gothic. A Baroque-style landscape park was constructed in the mid-eighteenth century, which was modified in the 1830s in an English garden style.

In September 1944, retreating German troops destroyed the interior of the castle, including its library, portrait collection, and furnishings.[33] This was the first blow in a cycle of decline that was to last many decades. Some restoration work began on the main building in the 1960s, but during these years nearby residents began using the castle as a source of construction materials and firewood.[34] Slowly, the materials of the building were disappearing, and it was becoming a ruin. In 2000, Bánffy Castle was included on the World Monuments Watch List of most endangered sites.

Yet something was beginning. A year prior, agreements between the Romanian Ministry of Culture and the Hungarian Ministry of Cultural Heritage initiated long-term conservation efforts. One of the first priorities was the restoration of the roof of the main building. This aligns with the strategy of priority repairs discussed in Chapter 4.

Although initial funds and efforts addressed some essential repairs, they were by no means sufficient to complete all the repairs and restoration needed at the castle complex. In the early 2000s, restoration and training courses began, and in 2005 a unique program was established that would incrementally restore the castle: the Built Heritage Conservation Training Centre.

Bánffy Castle, 2006. (Andrei Kokelburg, CC BY-SA 3.0 RO <https://creativecommons.org/licenses/by-sa/3.0/ro/deed.en>, via Wikimedia Commons)

Built Heritage Conservation training courses are offered at the castle in multiple sessions each year. The courses are open to university students in fields such as architecture, engineering, archaeology, and art history as well as craftspeople and tradespeople who specialize in historic buildings. Participants learn and practice hands-on conservation techniques at the complex on a range of materials from wood to stone. Around the world, there are similar initiatives. In the United States, for example, the Historic Preservation Training Center works to build trade skills while incrementally restoring heritage sites of the National Park Service.

The Built Heritage Conservation training courses at Bánffy Castle also help stimulate the local economy. Materials for the conservation are bought locally, and there are food and accommodation opportunities for the students and the visitors who come for the music and film festivals. "Ever since the castle restoration began, and especially due to the events organised here, there is a growing friendliness, cooperation, and a sense of pride with the local village," says Zsuzsanna Eke, an art historian who works with the Transylvania Trust. "The local council proudly uses the name and image of the castle and they talk about their heritage and the attractiveness of their living environment."[35]

Carpentry training at the Built Heritage Conservation Heritage Training Centre, 2021. (Transylvania Trust)

Stone masonry training at the Built Heritage Conservation Training Centre, 2022. (Transylvania Trust)

The goal of the Built Heritage Conservation Training program, says the Transylvania Trust, is the complete restoration of the castle, "carried out using traditional methods and materials, through international collaboration and an exemplary cooperation between designers and executors"[36] as a model of sustainable development through built heritage.

Children's summer camp in Bánffy Castle, 2023. (Transylvania Trust)

Bánffy Castle, 2024. (Lepedus-Sikso Péter/Transylvania Trust)

Rural vernacular architecture and the building process: women replastering an adobe house in Chamisal, New Mexico. Photo by Russell Lee, 1940. (Library of Congress, Prints & Photographs Division, FSA/OWI Collection [LC-USF34- 037082-D (P&P) LOT 628 (corresponding photographic print)])

Of course, incremental or cyclical repair work on buildings is not a new concept. Traditional buildings around the world, especially those made of adobe, mud bricks, and compressed earth, need cyclical maintenance that is usually a collective activity. This ongoing renewal becomes part of the living heritage of the community. In Mali, West Africa, for example, traditional mud brick buildings such as the Great Mosque of Djenné need annual repair, which becomes a ceremonial tradition enacted by generations of masons.[37] In the United States, examples of traditional craft skills include adobe construction and timber barn raising. Around the world, these traditional techniques are strongly linked with community.

Yet traditional construction techniques are being lost and supplanted, most often by the ubiquitous concrete. Local construction and decoration

techniques that take time and generational know-how are slipping away. This has led to a resurgence of efforts to preserve and adapt traditional techniques.

The ongoing works at Bánffy Castle through the training courses contribute to its incremental restoration. Each year, more of the restoration is completed with participation from people from all over the world. In 2024, the program focused on the former carriage house, and once that is completed, all the buildings of the castle will once more be under a roof. As participants draw together to work on the site and interact with each other and the local community, human connections are also built, reinforcing the social role of enduring heritage structures.

Raising last half of gable end panel into place on a barn. Southeast Missouri Farms Project. Photo by Russell Lee, 1938. (Library of Congress, Prints & Photographs Division, FSA/OWI Collection [LC-USF33-011535-M5 (b&w film nitrate neg.) LC-DIG-fsa-8a23180 (digital file from original neg.)])

Individuation: Denny Row Housing (Pittsburgh, Pennsylvania, US)

Denny Row is a block of nine brick Victorian-style townhomes built by Harmar D. Denny in 1888–1889 on the North Side of Pittsburgh, Pennsylvania (US).[38] The three-story homes were built as investment rental properties in the developing neighborhood and were owned by the Denny family through the 1920s. Subsequent owners converted the large townhouses into boarding houses to profit from the market for low-cost single-room housing for the working class. Absentee landlords remained a problem for the neighborhood for the ensuing decades.

In 1992, over a hundred years after the townhomes were built, members of the Allegheny West Civic Council (AWCC), a nonprofit citizens' group that had formed in the neighborhood in the mid-1970s, focused on the redevelopment of the Denny Row block. At that point, the connected townhomes had been vacant for about fifteen years. According to a history of Pittsburgh's North Side, Denny Row's corner of the neighborhood in the 1990s was an area that "many had assumed beyond hope."[39] The rundown Denny Row was a dominant presence in its neighborhood.

And yet the buildings were not beyond saving. Despite some vandalism during the years of abandonment, many of the interiors retained original features such as plaster crown moldings, slate mantels that had been painted to look like marble, and oak staircases. The problem was the scale of the project. Individual homeowners and their potential financiers would hesitate to invest in the rehabilitation of one of the structures when the rest of the block remained abandoned, and the townhomes needed a lot of work. The risk was too high.

AWCC had a creative epiphany and approached funders with a proposal: to support their exterior rehabilitation of the entire row as a shell, leaving the interior restoration and fit-out to the homeowners. This approach is often called an envelope rehabilitation. The shell or envelope approach should not be confused with another approach, called façadism, which occurs when the façade of a historic building is retained while the remainder of the building is demolished for a new structure behind the façade.

Façadism typically takes place in locations where development pressure is extremely high, such as commercial city centers. It's often criticized as a practice that reduces the historic façade to a sham, with little relation to its new context. AWCC's intention was that the historic integrity of the townhomes be retained because they viewed it as an asset to the neighborhood and potential homebuyers.

Scaffolding and shadows on the façace of the Fine Arts building on Grand Circus Park in Detroit, which has been awaiting redevelopment for fifteen years, 2024. (Amy Hetletvedt)

One of the Denny Row townhomes in 1990, before renovation. (Courtesy of Mary Callison estate, via Rachel Callison)

Denny Row with the AWCC banner advertising the upcoming work, circa mid-1990s. (Courtesy of Mary Callison estate, via Rachel Callison)

The shell technique is more analogous to Elemental's half-house projects or the spirit of John Turner's work. The arrangement kept the overall cost of the renovation lower and focused the professional expertise on the more complex exterior and structural renovations. The nature of the interior fit-out empowered homeowners to develop new skills and shape their own living spaces, hiring their own architects and contractors for the interior work.[40]

AWCC assembled a team of architects and engineers to survey the townhomes and draft plans for the shell rehabilitation. Through a competitive bid process, a contractor was selected. While the shell rehabilitation was taking

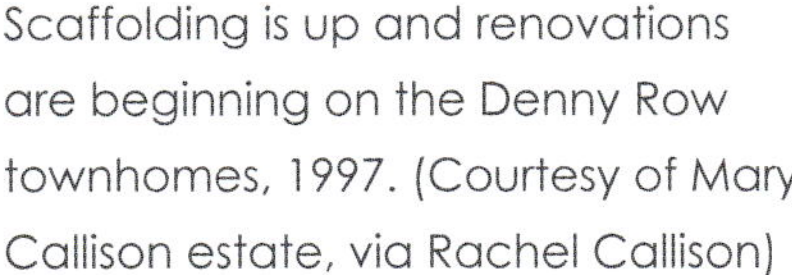

Scaffolding is up and renovations are beginning on the Denny Row townhomes, 1997. (Courtesy of Mary Callison estate, via Rachel Callison)

Work begins on the interior of a Denny Row townhome, 1998. (Courtesy of Mary Callison estate, via Rachel Callison)

place, AWCC began marketing the townhomes and partnered with financing institutions to assist potential buyers. Over the next ten years, all but one of the townhomes were purchased and their interiors were completed. The final home in the row was purchased, renovated, and sold between 2021 and 2023.[41] Says John Martine, an architect involved with the project, "The historic restoration of these row houses' facades inspired new, individual home ownership."[42]

Thirty years later, several of the Denny Row townhomes remain in the families of those who bought in during the shell project years, fostering a strong sense of neighborhood identity, pride, and longevity within the community. Allegheny West is the smallest official neighborhood in Pittsburgh. Denny Row—along with Emmanuel Episcopal Church—stabilized two of the neighborhood's border streets.

Through the patience and vision of residents, both established and incoming, the Denny Row homes reflect collaboration and incremental redevelopment. The shell technique is a practical approach that reflects the benefits of individuation, creating a collage in time.

Exterior of Denny Row townhomes after renovation, circa 1998. (Courtesy John A. Martine, architect)

A Denny Row townhome porch after renovation, circa 1998. (Courtesy John A. Martine, architect)

PART III

Community Examples: Profiles of Purpose

Table set for Soul Food Dinner at Dorchester Projects (Archive House), 2012. (Photo by Eric Allix Rogers)

Chapter 7

Radical Hospitality

Chicago: Dorchester Projects and Stony Island Arts Bank

Chicago, Illinois, US (Greater Grand Crossings Neighborhood)
Featured Time Period: 2006–2015

Inside a two-story frame house on Chicago's South Side, a meal is being served. There's a clink of dishes, mouthwatering smells. Every seat at the long table is filled. Every plate and palate ready. It's Soul Food Pavilion at the Archive House, one of three structures on Dorchester Street renovated by artist Theaster Gates in the early 2000s. Soul Food Pavilion is a community event that Gates coordinated in 2012, which brought together friends and strangers for a shared meal around long plank tables set with candles and pottery made by Gates.

"The dinners give, for me—they give me an opportunity to leverage ritual, to ask hard questions maybe in ways that people don't normally talk about in Chicago; with groups of people who don't normally get together," said Gates of the event,[1] which included culinary explanations by the chefs, a performance by musical group The Black Monks, and impromptu remarks from participants.

> *"Hospitality as an art form honors the communal as an arena for transformation."*
> *—Maria Fee*

Conversation during Soul Food Dinner at Dorchester Projects (Archive House), 2012. (Photo by Eric Allix Rogers)

Soul Food Pavilion was part of a University of Chicago Smart Museum series of events subtitled Radical Hospitality.[2] Artist and theologian Maria Fee, in the context of discussing Gates's work, said, "Hospitality as an art form honors dwelling as a mode of aesthetic contemplation, the potentiality of neglected neighborhoods, and the communal as an arena for transformation."[3] For the Soul Food Pavilion meal, Gates invited city residents from near and far to dine together. In a video about the project, Gates defines his approach to radical hospitality this way: "What does it mean for us to share the abundance of generosity that we have with other people?"[4]

His approach to renovations of three structures on Dorchester Street can be viewed in the same light as his approach to the dinner: opening a way for the buildings to be generous with their space. He invited abandoned or distressed buildings into usefulness and hospitality. "I sometimes think it is not enough to be concerned with just the restoration of a building," he says. "I also try to think about what needs it will serve. So I become an advocate for these existing buildings, and instead of just restoring them, I create a program for them that makes them more valuable than they've ever been to their community."[5]

Gates's first purchase in the South Side community was a single-story commercial building, a former candy store. The house next door became available for $16,000, a fallout of the global financial crisis of 2007–2008, which increased vacancy in a neighborhood that was already under socioeconomic strain from decades of disinvestment. He purchased a third home on the corner of the block in 2009. Gates financed these projects on an individual and informal level, purchasing some structures himself and others with loans and gifts from friends and former co-workers.[6]

Gates programmed the spaces as repositories for cultural resources that were being divested. The former candy store became the home of a collection of vinyl records from Dr. Wax Records, a record store whose Hyde Park outlet closed in 2010. The second became the Archive House, accommodating the 14,000-volume collection of the shuttered Prairie Avenue bookstore and 60,000 glass lantern slides that had been archived at the University of Chicago. The third house initially became the Black Cinema House, which held screenings and filmmaking classes. Gates has the gift of seeing the value in discarded resources—collections cast aside because they are viewed as obsolete or analog.

Material collections shape the stories we tell in the built environment. As bulldozers and wrecking balls chewed their way through Detroit, I had

The former candy store as the Listening House, with the Archive House visible at the right, 2011. (Photo by Eric Allix Rogers)

a persistent urge to rescue some of the objects of daily living that were on a pipeline to landfill because I felt that these objects had a powerful human connection to the history of the city, situating human lives in place and time.

In 2014, the Victoria and Albert Museum in England recognized a new category of activity called rapid response collecting. Although the museum focuses on design and manufacturing, there is overlap with social and humanitarian issues. The museum's growing rapid response collection includes an umbrella from the umbrella protest movement in Hong Kong in 2014 and the refugee flag designed in 2016, based on the fabric of life jackets.

As mentioned in Chapter 5, author Orhan Pamuk filled a nineteenth-century building in Istanbul with objects and artifacts that he had collected to write the novel *The Museum of Innocence* and opened it to the public as a museum of the same name in 2012. In a "Museum Manifesto," Pamuk says, "The measure of a museum's success should not be its ability to represent a state, a nation or company, or a particular history. It should be its capacity to reveal the humanity of individuals. . . . If objects are not uprooted from their environs and their streets, but are situated with care and ingenuity in their natural homes, they will already portray their own stories."[7]

While Gates kept and curated some of the materials and collections in the Chicago community, he also exported materials from some projects to

The Archive House is clad with salvaged wood, 2012. (Photo by Eric Allix Rogers)

finance others. Gates fabricated sculptures from the debris of the renovated Dorchester houses, which sold for up to $120,000 each.[8] Before the restoration of the Black Cinema House, Gates salvaged architectural elements from the house to Kassel, Germany, so that they could enter into a "visual and historical conversation"[9] with the nineteenth-century Huguenot House in the exhibit Documenta(13).[10]

In his work, Gates acknowledged what writer John Colapinto called a "mutually exploitative transaction"[11] to fund neighborhood rebuilding projects. The whole-house extraction of the White House project by Ryan Mendoza, discussed in Chapter 1, provoked local outrage in Detroit. Further reflection on the motivations, reactions, and outcomes of these material extractions in Chicago, Detroit, and elsewhere can contribute to a larger dialogue about when extractive practices are helpful and when they are hurtful.[12]

Gates seems to view the entire neighborhood not only as source but also as fuel in an ongoing cycle of creativity. In a 2013 *New York Times* maga-

A room in the Theaster Gates's *12 Ballads for Huguenot House* at Documenta13, 2012. (© Nils Klinger)

zine article, Ben Austen writes, "Gates believes that this is almost the work of art—identifying talented people who can benefit from the 'off-heating' of his projects, empowering them, figuring out how they can help maintain and enlarge a community of innovation, enterprise and security. 'I'm creating a kind of ecology of opportunity,' he says."[13]

Gates and his creative ideas were charismatic sparks that attracted other creatives and stakeholders. Marlease Bushnell, a staff member in Gates's studio, discussing a 2013 artist retreat, said of Gates's leadership, "We know it's Theaster's gig. We know he'll get the credit. But he gives you agency. 'Here's your lane,' he says. 'You run with it.'"[14]

Around the corner from the Dorchester projects is the Stony Island Trust and Savings Bank, designed by William Gibbons Uffendell, built in 1923. The three-story, 17,000-square-foot brick and terracotta building anchors the corner of 68th Street and Stony Island Avenue, one of the South Side's major north–south thoroughfares.

The Stony Island Trust and Savings Bank was out of business less than a decade after its construction because of the stock market crash and ensuing

The Stony Island Arts Bank before its renovation in an undated photo. (Cook County GIS Records [Photo ID:919370])

economic depression. It housed a series of banks in the following years, but the Greek Revival temple-style building was vacant by the 1980s. After decades of vacancy, the building was scheduled for demolition in 2012.

The recognition that Gates and the Rebuild Foundation (established by Gates in 2010) had earned through their work in the community caught the attention of City Hall. Inspired by a visit to the Dorchester Projects, then-Chicago mayor Rahm Emanuel asked Gates what he could do to help. The city offered the Rebuild Foundation the opportunity to purchase the vacant bank building for $1, with stipulations about safety and stabilization.

The repairs that had to be completed by the Rebuild Foundation before the project could begin are an example of the priority approaches discussed in Chapter 4. At the Stony Island Bank, preliminary work was needed to fix the leaky roof, reanchor some of the terracotta pieces, and secure the building from entry.[15] If these essential repairs had not been addressed, the building would have deteriorated further, with less of the original material to preserve.

Gates described the initial financing stage of the project:

> The bank didn't have institutional support. There was no money in the TIF (Tax Increment Financing), there is no foot traffic to say that if we build a restaurant or anything here that there's a local community that's

A vacant bank building on Detroit's East Side, 2006. (Amy Hetletvedt)

A bank building converted for use as a church on Detroit's East Side, 2006. (Amy Hetletvedt)

> going to support it. And as a result of all those things that I couldn't create a pro forma around, it was very hard to get the party started. So the [Stony Island] bank really needed creative solutions. It meant I had to put some skin in the game. I had to find alternative ways of generating revenue, and then once people saw that I was for real, and that I have a track record now, they thought, "Ok, we'll support half the investment." There's a group called the Chicago Community Loan Fund that specializes in financing high-risk projects in poor communities—they make their money off CRAs (Community Reinvestment Act) and bank tax credits—and they became a partner.[16]

The Rebuild Foundation saw the potential of the building as a hub for its cultural collections and arts programming. But perhaps an additional reason that Gates identified it as an important building from "Day One"[17] is its potential for narrative and critical commentary.

The closing of bank branches was a symptom of the broader disinvestment the community experienced in the latter half of the twentieth century, when the population was predominantly African American.[18] This story of disinvestment became a story that this project could tell. And the bank was the perfect mouthpiece.

Like Detroit, Chicago is dotted with corner bank buildings from the 1920s and 1930s. Because of their sturdy materials and construction, these struc-

The interior of the Archive House on Dorchester, housing the collection of books from Prairie Avenue Books, 2012. (Photo by Eric Allix Rogers)

The library at the Stony Island Arts Bank, including the collection of the Johnson Publishing Archive, 2024. (Amy Hetletvedt)

tures have withstood years of inattention. Virtually none of them continue to be occupied as banks. Many have become hair salons, furniture stores, restaurants, or churches. Many stand vacant.

The bank buildings of this era are usually composed of the visual language of Greek and Roman temples. The classical elements—ionic columns, arches, pediments—were used by the original designers to convey solidity, a cultural continuity with antiquity. In essence, they were temples to the financial system. But in distressed communities, the same financial systems failed their neighborhoods through discriminatory lending practices such as redlining and blockbusting (inducing panic selling by appealing to fears related to minorities moving in, then profiting from turnover).

The building's reprogramming as an arts center poetically capitalized on this irony by recontextualizing bank symbols and materials in a cultural repository, recasting familiar visual and cultural symbols to introduce a question or to tell a different story. The Stony Island Arts Bank examines the idea of a bank and a bank's function in a community. What are we saving? What are we "banking on"? What are we investing in? What is true wealth?

Gates expressed this idea in a fundraising tool that he devised for the project. He cut one hundred marble slabs from the interior of the bank building and engraved them with wording similar to that on bank bonds. In the center of the bonds, next to an image of the Stony Island bank building, are the words "In Art We Trust."

Gates first exhibited the Stony Island bond at Art Basel in Switzerland, a world-renowned art show in the world's seat of finance. "You know, development is an action to me," said Gates. "I believe that beautiful things should happen in my neighborhood and that action requires these mechanisms. . . . But there are also some things that I can do as an artist that developers can't do, like I'll create a bank bond for the bank and have the bank pay for itself, and that's poetic to me."[19] Gates sold the bonds at $5,000 each to raise capital for the restoration.[20]

The Stony Island Arts Bank project demonstrates that one element of community revitalization is through banking on, if you will, a community's cultural resources. The Arts Bank houses prominent collections such as the archive of Johnson Publishing, which published *Ebony* and *Jet* magazines, and the glass lantern slides that were moved from the Archive House.

The Stony Island Arts Bank was added to the National Register of Historic Places in 2013, and the project met the standards of the Secretary of the Interior's Standards for Rehabilitation. It's arguable that the preservation of this cornerstone building was enabled by cultural resource activation and rehabilitation of the smaller, neighborhood structures such as the Dorchester Houses over the preceding decade, because they demonstrated value over time. This project exemplifies the neighborhood-scaled incremental process discussed in Chapter 3. Gates says, "Instead of building 40,000-square-foot cultural centers or large YMCAs or big new libraries, couldn't we use some of the existing housing stock and make better, more thoughtful incremental decisions?"[20]

Various aspects of the creative interventions in the South Side Chicago neighborhood demonstrate the three purposeful approaches described in this book: priority, poetic, and practical. Through these creative endeavors and his visionary way of seeing, Gates (and the Rebuild Foundation) reused and recontextualized materials to create something new. Over a decade, interventions into multiple structures in the neighborhood, including other projects such as the Dorchester Housing and Arts Collaborative, have fostered a place where neighborhood residents, artists, scholars, curators, and collectors come together to engage with its history.

The remains of the arched plaster ceiling and bank clock over the bank-lobby-turned-gallery at the Stony Island Arts Bank, 2024. (Amy Hetletvedt)

A postcard of the Electrical Building at the World's Columbian Exposition of 1893, constructed not far from what is now the Stony Island Arts Bank. The Chicago Architecture Center notes that the neoclassical buildings, as "temples to industry and civilization," became templates for banks and public buildings across the country." (Library of Congress, Prints & Photographs Division. Winters Art Lithographing Company. Electrical building. World's Columbian Exposition, ca. 1892. Oct. 29. Reproduction number LC-DIG-pga-03063)

Two of the modified buildings on Dorchester Street among their neighbors, 2024. (Amy Hetletvedt)

The Stony Island Arts Bank soon after its reopening in 2015. (Jeff Zoline)

"Every day we are in conversation with our neighbors. Some people are excited about it, others are maybe just glad something is happening to all the waste land. And others just assume I am a front for some corporation," says Gates.[22] "I may not have the money to restore the entire South Side of Chicago," he said a few years prior, "but I do have the capacity to help people re-imagine what the South Side could be."[23] It's a work in progress, and the processes of making, of dialogue, and of sharing—whether meals or pottery or renovated buildings—are an investment yielding compound interest.

The Remembrance Structure glows on a starry night, circa 2018.
(Courtesy Reid Freeman)

Chapter 8

A Different Story to Tell

Rural Virginia: Menokin and Remembrance Structure

Location: Warsaw, Virginia, USA
Featured time period: 1940–2023

It's dusk at a former plantation in the rural community of Warsaw, on Virginia's Northern Neck, and a gathering is breaking up. Hugs. Quiet talk. Farewells. Purses and bags retrieved and slung from shoulders. The crunch of gravel under tires as cars pull away.

As human sounds recede, nature sounds emerge—the hum of cicadas and the rising melody of spring frogs. Bunches of cut carnations glow white at the base of trees and at corners of posts long buried, some of which have been unearthed.

The posts supported cabins, the carnations are a memorial, and the people gathered at the site were descendants of the enslaved people who built the plantation's structures and were forced to work on its lands for nearly a century.

Most of the cabin corners are marked only with stakes. But atop four of the stakes is a new simple wood-framed structure. It's wrapped in translucent screen, and as nightfall comes, the empty box begins to glow, illuminated from within. It's called the Remembrance Structure.

The former quarters for enslaved people and the smaller utilitarian buildings flanked an axis leading to the home built for the owner of the eighteenth-century tobacco plantation. Darkness falls thick and heavy in the Virginia tidewater region, and in the morning light, the plantation house can be seen for what it is: a ruin. Tumble-down masonry and stunted chimneys. Only two corners of the house are true and standing.

This structure is Menokin, a name retained from the Algonquin name for the place.[1] It was commissioned in 1769 for Francis Lightfoot Lee, one of the signatories of the American Declaration of Independence, and his new bride, Rebecca Tayloe. The home and the site have become a multilayered effort to tell the story not only of the building—its construction techniques, disrepair, and the technical aspects of its repair—but also of the people involved with the building, including the enslaved laborers who built the house and worked the land.

Made of red sandstone, Menokin's walls received a coat of stucco in the early nineteenth century. Although they have since collapsed, the house originally had a central arched doorway and a symmetrical arrangement of windows. The original architect is unknown, but the design is influenced by European classical ideals, particularly those of sixteenth-century Italian architect Andrea Palladio.[2]

Menokin, Frances Benjamin Johnston, photographer. Photo taken circa 1930–1939. (Frances Benjamin Johnston Photograph Collection, Library of Congress, Prints & Photographs Division. Reproduction number [LC-DIG-csas-05541])

Menokin door, Frances Benjamin Johnston, photographer. Photo taken circa 1930–1939. (Frances Benjamin Johnston Photograph Collection, Library of Congress, Prints & Photographs Division. Reproduction number [LC-DIG-csas-05541])

The end of the American Civil War in 1865 radically changed an economy that depended on enforced human labor as its engine. Thus, the Menokin plantation's second century of existence—from the 1860s to the 1960s—was very different from its first. Because Francis Lightfoot Lee died in 1797 without a direct heir, the house changed hands multiple times in the late nineteenth and early twentieth centuries. It was last occupied sometime in the mid-twentieth century and fell into a state of abandon, eventually leading to the collapse of sections of its walls.

In recognition of the house's significance and its precarious state, the house was originally documented by the Historic American Building Survey (HABS) in the late 1930s. This process produced measured drawings and photographs of the house, which became invaluable to later efforts. Documentation is featured under the priority approach for endangered or threatened structures (Chapter 4). Although documentation does not repair anything on a building or steer an outcome, it's a technique that is beneficial for vacant or distressed buildings that have been identified as significant by preservationists or community members but don't have immediate potential for renovation.[3]

In the mid-1960s, three architectural history students from the University of Virginia heard about Menokin and decided to make the trip of just over 100 miles east. Student Calder Loth recalls finding the house this way: "Sure enough, there was Menokin, wide open. At that time, it was completely intact, although it was in very neglected condition. All of the woodwork was there, all of the paneling, and that was in a relatively good state of preservation even though it was getting no maintenance."[4]

HABS photo of Menokin after a partial collapse, circa 1998. Jack E. Boucher, photographer. (Library of Congress, Prints & Photographs Division, HABS. Reproduction number [HABS VA,80-WAR.V,6-])

But a repeat visit a few years later revealed something more heartbreaking than hopeful. A tree had fallen and partially collapsed the structure, and all the original interior woodwork was gone.

Decades passed. By the 1980s, Loth was employed as an architectural historian in Virginia's Department of Historic Resources. He was contacted by one of Menokin's co-owners, who was concerned about a notification about the home's potential loss of its National Historic Landmark Status[5] due to its deteriorating condition.

As Loth tried to drum up support and envision potential solutions for Menokin, a small coalition developed. Martin King, a retired executive who lived in the area and was also concerned about Menokin, became instrumental in shepherding the project. Another site visit and a chance meeting with Edgar Omohundro and the other co-owner of the site revealed some wonderful news: The wood paneling had not been stolen. Omohundro told the visitors that he had removed the woodwork in 1966 because he couldn't secure Menokin and had stored the pieces in a nearby unoccupied house.

In 1995, after Omohundro's co-owner passed away, he donated the house ruin and 500 acres of the original plantation to the newly established Menokin Foundation to ensure its preservation. The first order of business for the Menokin Foundation was to accept the donation and undertake the stabilization of the remaining ruins.

The Menokin interior woodwork in storage at another site, circa 1985. (© Menokin Foundation)

The steel canopy over the Menokin ruin, 2023. (© Menokin Foundation)

A steel roof structure was erected over the home's remains, an example of a priority approach for endangered or threatened structures. The roof canopy, completed in 2000 with grant funding from the Commonwealth of Virginia,[6] protects the remaining building fabric from further deterioration from weather.

The steps that were taken over the decades to preserve the structure, including saving the woodwork and erecting the steel canopy, not only retained critical historic fabric but helped to tell a story. And the story is what ultimately propelled the project forward.

In the early 2000s, grading at the site revealed evidence of cabins. An Advisory Council, formed in 2009 of interested conservators and architects and later the foundation's board, grappled with a question: What should or could be done with the deteriorating plantation house and its site, a home that spoke to the birth of our country and its ideals but whose very form bore witness to inherent contradictions of these ideals?

From these questions, several purposes emerged, which correspond with the purposes described in Chapter 2: to steward the site and landscape (environmental benefits), to use the house as a teaching tool (practical benefits), and to tell the story of the site and its people (poetic benefits).

Menokin has been a site of human occupation for centuries. The sites of Native American habitation offer opportunities for archaeological investigation. Intense genealogical research has identified descendants of Menokin's enslaved workers and servants, and many of these descendants have attended on-site events, such as the gathering described at this chapter's opening. Study of the landscape is yet to be undertaken: How were the fields arranged in the eighteenth and early nineteenth centuries? What crops were grown here? Where were the barns and other farm buildings located?

Graduate student Meghan O'Connor explained the practical benefit of the approach taken toward the plantation house: "Incredibly, about 80% of Menokin's original materials survived, including much of the interior woodwork. Martin King, founding President of the Menokin Foundation, saw a unique preservation opportunity—that Menokin could be a more informative teaching tool disassembled."[7]

Journalist Michael J. Lewis said that the idea of using the structure as a teaching tool "casts a new light on the surviving woodwork, some of it surely made by slave labor. It is strangely expressive in its dismantled state, showing exquisite finish on one side and the crude gouges of the adze on the other, speaking of ceremony and formality, but also of labor. To reinstall the paneling in a re-created house would immediately make it less interesting."[8]

The foundation engaged the architecture firm Machado Silvetti to develop an architectural vision for the house's future. The firm's design includes a structural glass envelope to reenclose the structure and the use of glass walkways and flooring inside the house so that the original construction methods of the house are visible. "By visually showing the process of reconstruction," says the foundation, "the story of Menokin will be told—not as a snapshot in time but as a continuing narrative—while serving as a powerful teaching tool."[9]

Menokin director of education Alice French explains Menokin's construction techniques to a group of visitors, 2021. (© Menokin Foundation)

The HABS documentation has proven invaluable as a guide to the form and appearance of the portions of the house that need to be reconstructed to provide a stable junction with the glass.

Lewis further described the teaching potential of the structure: "For one thing, the ruin itself presented an unusual opportunity, for the standing portions were astonishingly well-preserved. For an 18th-century house to survive with just two coats of interior paint is unheard of. The tree that sliced it open laid bare a fascinating cross-section of stucco, stone, brick and plaster. Here was a compendium of 18th-century building trades—bricklaying and stone-cutting, carpentry and joinery, plastering and glazing. All is peeled apart as in a scientific dissection and will remain visible as Machado Silvetti's glass wall begins where Menokin's jagged stone wall ends."[10] And, as Lewis also pointed out, the glass wall will allow viewers to perceive both sides of the story: the smooth careful finish of the wood paneling on one side and the marks of its making on the other.

At the excavation site of one of the cabins, another opportunity for narrative benefit emerged: the new structure discussed at the opening of this chapter, now known as the Remembrance Structure. When little or none of the original fabric of a historic structure remains, one of several approved treatment options included in the US Secretary of the Interior's Standards for

The corner of a historic house on Mackinac Island, Michigan, is cut away and covered in glass so that visitors can see the construction below. (Amy Hetletvedt)

The concept rendering for the Glass House project at Menokin reveals a similar concept at a larger scale. (© Machado Silvetti)

Treatments of Historic Properties is reconstruction, re-creating a structure as it existed in a specific period of history.

Architect Reid Freeman's design called for reconstructing the timber framing of the cabin, which was based on research of nearby surviving structures and their material and methods. But he chose not to reconstruct any other parts of the cabin. Instead, the timber framing is wrapped in a translucent building membrane—an entirely new and nonhistorical choice.

Says Freeman, "The membrane protects the wood framing from the elements and provides comfortable daylight levels to the interior. At night, solar powered interior flood lamps highlight the structure's tectonics and the structure serves as a luminous memorial to the site's forgotten history and inhabitants."[11]

Framing the timber for the Remembrance Structure, 2018. (Courtesy Reid Freeman)

The translucent membrane over the Remembrance Structure, 2018. (Courtesy Reid Freeman)

In other words, the creative nonhistoric Remembrance Structure serves the site's interpretive purposes better as an abstracted memorial, which evocatively links to the site's story, than as a historical object. This decision opened up alternative paths of experience and interpretation.

Tom Duckenfield, a former Menokin trustee and descendant of one of the enslaved people at the site, said that the Remembrance Structure's illumination at night "conjures up for me things which the descendant community can appreciate as well. At night, after work was done, oftentimes those who were enslaved would meet, with the backdrop of a woodsy atmosphere or a forest and have religious services. And you could identify these places because they would be illuminated by whatever they were using for light."[12]

The restoration and reconstruction of the house as required are proceeding according to the US Secretary of the Interior's Standards, and because it is a registered Virginia Historic Landmark, treatments are monitored by the state's preservation office. Phase 1A of the project, the rebuilding of the southwest corner of the ruin, was completed in October 2022. Fundraising for Phase 1B, the final stabilization phase before the steel and glass phases begin, is ongoing as of the writing of this book. The unique reconstruction of Menokin will take at least several years. This pace allows the reconstruction process to become an exhibition in itself and a hands-on teaching tool. An important part of Menokin's education mission is to engage student interns to assist and learn from the work.

Beyond the value of the plantation house as an educational platform, the 500-acre site has social and environmental value as an outdoor recreation site and a haven for wildlife. "Menokin has been nourishing people for millennia," says Calder Loth, the former student who has now been involved in the project for almost sixty years.[13] The site has been designated an Indigenous cultural landscape because it retains the natural and cultural resources that supported Indigenous populations.[14] The majority of the site is part of the Rappahanock River Valley Wildlife Refuge. Kayaking and birdwatching are some of the outdoor activities hosted on site.

Menokin and its site, from the point of its abandonment in the mid-twentieth century to the partial completion of the Glass House project as of the writing of this book, has been evolving to tell a broader story. The story is not only about a founding father but about the overarching history of site, of the house and its material construction, of the people who were forced to build it and work the land, and the changes that come with the sweep of time. As

An aerial shot of Menokin landscape, early 2000s, showing the Menokin ruins and canopy in the context of their landscape. (© Menokin Foundation)

architect Reid Freeman says, "the strength of Menokin is the willingness to tell the story of everything."[15]

> "The strength is the willingness to tell the story of everything."
> —Reid Freeman

Similar techniques to those used at Menokin can be seen elsewhere in the world: in the canopy over the Casa Grande Ruins in Arizona, in Richard Nickel's beautifully haunting documentation of the disappearing buildings in Chicago (profiled in Chapter 4), and even various approaches to ruined manor houses such as Astley Castle in England, which was achieved—it should be noted—in part because of a flattening of the triangle-based delivery model. The architects and the clients were one and the same.[16]

In its unflinching honesty about the disinvested years, Menokin is an example for others looking to find a way forward with distressed buildings and sites. Loth says, "We feel that even though this [the Glass House] might look kind of strange, that it does promote curiosity and interest about an important part of Menokin's history. And it tells that the house went into a period of decline and abandonment and collapsed. And we're graphically displaying that part of its history by not putting Menokin back exactly as it was, but by putting the missing pieces of the walls back in glass. We have to

The Astley Castle in Warwickshire, England, demonstrates an alternative technique to the glass house proposed at Menokin with new walls inserted within the old. Photo 2014. (Greg Storrar, CC BY-SA 3.0 <https://creativecommons.org/licenses/by-sa/3.0> via Wikimedia Commons)

The shed roof at Casa Grande ruins in Arizona (seen as a black canopy with columns visible behind) is similar in concept to the shed over Menokin's ruins. Photo documentation compiled after 1933. (Library of Congress, Prints & Photographs Division, HABS, Reproduction number HABS ARIZ,11-COOL.V,1-)

make Menokin interesting for the future. Just having another historic house really isn't needed. We have a different story to tell."[17]

The Menokin site's interventions—some of which were banal and practical, others creative and inventive—developed incrementally over many years while the site's future was uncertain. As writer Michael J. Lewis puts it, this has shaped the site into "neither ruin nor replica but something in between."[18]

The Granby Winter Garden, Cairns Street, Liverpool, England, 2019. (Audrey Walker Images/Alamy Stock Photo)

Chapter 9

Service Is Your Rent

Liverpool: 10 Houses on Cairns Street and Granby Winter Garden

Location: Liverpool, England, UK
Featured time period: 1993–2019

As a breeze blows through the brick shell of an empty Victorian terraced house in England's industrial north, leaves and climbing tendrils rustle. Trees and plants of varied species—some in pots and some planted firmly in the earth—luxuriate in the morning sun.

Echoes of neighbors greeting each other and friendly chatter are muted by the same verdant leaves. What the community has spent years planting and tending has taken firm root. This is the Granby Winter Garden, a garden for a community that has come through a long winter.

Like many urban neighborhoods, the Toxteth community of Liverpool, England (otherwise known as Liverpool 8) began experiencing disinvestment, economic decline, and population loss in the late 1960s. Riots in Toxteth in 1981, which ignited after the arrest of Leroy Cooper, a young Black man, accelerated the abandonment of the built environment. At least seventy buildings were demolished or burned down as a result of the riots, which began at the corner of Granby and Selborne streets.[1]

Community members formed the Granby Residents Association in 1993 to try to prevent the demolition of the area's remaining Victorian terraced houses[2] (what may be called a townhouse in the United States, a multistory structure with shared walls on two sides). The association worked to envision and advocate for alternatives to demolition of empty properties.

Organizing and advocacy was a big part of it, but caretaking became the greater part. Leroy Cooper, the man whose arrest sparked the Toxteth riots, went on to become a photographer and to document struggles and resilience in Liverpool. He spoke of this caretaking attitude in 2023, the year of his death: "Service to others is the rent you pay for your room here on earth," he said. "We think sometimes that poverty is only being hungry, naked, and homeless. The poverty of being unwanted, unloved, and uncared for is the greatest poverty."[3]

Over many years, residents claimed and cared for the common exterior areas of the approximately one hundred abandoned and boarded houses in the area.[4] Boarding up and protecting a vacant home, or mothballing, is a pri-

Granby neighborhood children showcase the colorful boardups and plantings, 2014. (Gary Calton)

ority strategy to retain buildings (discussed in Chapter 4). Residents undertook painting, removing debris, and gardening. Lots of gardening. They planted fruits and vegetables in the front gardens of vacant properties and climbing vines on the walls. According to long-time resident Hazel Tilley, "The gardening was absolutely critical to getting people to move in."[5]

Alley gardens in Granby with Tigger the Boxer. (Hazel Tilley)

In the early 2000s, the terraced houses were again threatened when the Housing Market Renewal Initiative, which aimed to lift house prices by de-densifying communities, identified the neighborhood as a potential site for demolition and redevelopment. Although ultimately funding was cut for the initiative, damage was done in Granby as more homes were emptied.

"When these houses were scheduled for demolition, what the Council does is strip out everything inside. So it's just the shell. And once they've done that, they put a big sticker on the door which says: 'Nothing of value.' And there's something about that . . . process which is truly enraging. Because it has systematically taken away what has value . . ., and then stamps it as worthless,"[6] expresses a resident in a short film about the Winter Garden and the Granby community. According to resident Hazel Tilley, the council even stripped the lead flashings off the empty houses to prevent them from being stolen.[7]

These residents describe a frustrating paradox of disinvestment: As resources leave and property prices plummet, and in some cases resources are actively extracted from the community, the community is labeled as being without value. The Granby Four community describes the aftermath of the 1981 riots as having "blighted the reputation of the region."[8]

Strong and visible community activity continued through these years despite the disbanding of the Granby Residents Association. In 2011, the Granby 4 Streets Community Land Trust formed.[9] A community land trust (CLT) is a nonprofit organization that holds land and develops it in a democratic process for the benefit of the community.[10] CLTs can play a strong role not only in redeveloping properties in a community but in maintaining affordability as the neighborhood changes.

The Granby 4 Streets CLT was able to purchase ten vacant terraced houses, some of the last remaining Victorian terraces in the vicinity, through one major donor (who lent them capital at zero percent interest) and a matching fund from a nonprofit. They envisioned affordable housing for the homes, half of which they sold and half of which they maintain as rentals. The homes for sale were subject to a covenant where the sale price is tied to wages in Liverpool, not to the housing market.[11] "We've also applied criteria to the sale which matches social criteria—a connection with the area, first-time buyer, in need of decent housing at an affordable price," explains resident Hazel Tilley.[12] In addition to keeping the housing affordable, the CLT wanted to renovate the homes in a sustainable way and to approach it incrementally to give the community more opportunity to be involved.

Aerial of the Granby Four neighborhood in 2024, with Dulcie Street in the foreground with Jermyn and Cairns beyond, showing incremental progress of regeneration. (Mark Waugh/Alamy Stock Photo)

Granby 4 Streets CLT chair Erika Rushton describes the process of selecting the design group Assemble Studio to join them in revitalizing the ten vacant homes. The other groups "just offered a total solution. Every house would be done, with no recognition of what people have crafted into their individual homes, or the value that people had invested in the street with planting and building furniture. Regeneration is always this blunt, abstract, over-professionalised thing. But Assemble have shown how it can be done differently, by making things that people can see, touch, understand and put together for themselves."[13]

The team at Assemble Studio developed the proposed interventions for the ten homes based on the "resourcefulness and DIY spirit that defines the streets. . . . The resourceful, creative actions of a group of residents were fundamental to finally bringing these streets out of dereliction and back into use.

Over two decades they cleared, planted, painted, and campaigned in order to reclaim their streets," said Assemble.[14] Through workshops with the community, the designers and residents created products for the renovation of the homes, such as ceramic tiles, mantelpieces, and door pulls. A ceramics studio, the Granby Workshop, was born through this process and remains in the community, producing architectural tiles, fixtures, and homewares.

Thus, some of the key visual pieces used to bring the homes back to life were generated from within the community. Thanks to the publicity from winning the 2015 Turner Prize (a British prize for artists), the workshop was able to expand the number of products that it could offer and ultimately became self-sustaining. The renovation of the ten homes on Cairns Street contributed to the wellbeing of the community through the incubation and development of the workshop and maintained affordable housing that honored the creative spirit of the community.

One of the workshop creations that wound its way back into Granby houses was door pulls, crafted from clay burnished in a barbeque filled with sawdust and seasoned with banana skins and pine needles. It's an example of how putting back a new piece (like the stitchwork metaphor discussed in Chapter 3) can be done in a way that links it back into the story of the community. "The result," says a Granby Workshop Catalog, "is a harvest of unique door knobs . . ., a precious addition."[15]

Photo of Granby catalog of door pulls, 2015. (*Granby Workshop Catalogue 2015*, published by the Granby Workshop. Developed in collaboration between the Granby Workshop, Assemble Studio, and the 10 House Project with the Granby 4 Streets CLT)

The restoration of the ten houses on Cairns Street was designed to be an incremental process, although the five years it took to complete seemed long to many involved. "Five years to do ten chuffing houses!," exclaimed Hazel Tilley.[16] In the case of the ten houses on Cairns, the incremental approach allowed participation by a broader group of people and embraced varied solutions over time.

Although none of the terraced houses are listed monuments with Historic England, Assemble Studio proposed very few changes to the Victorian character of the exteriors. Brick was repaired, windows replaced in kind, roofs repaired with tiles like their neighbors. The interiors generally retained the original layout and room proportions, although the interiors have a much more modern and spare aesthetic than Queen Victoria might have preferred.

The Granby Winter Garden project was an idea conceived by the CLT and Assemble Studio together, based on design ideas drawn up during the renovations of the ten houses. Assemble adapted the idea for two other badly deteriorated terraced homes, which had much less original material to work with than the ten houses on Cairns. The roofs and floors had collapsed, windows and doors were missing, and the interior finish had worn away, leaving brickwork exposed.

The solution proposed for the Granby Winter Garden first took a priority approach. Essential repairs were needed to stabilize the structure. A horizontal blue steel band at the vertical midpoint braces the party walls. A new glazed roof prevents further deterioration. These interventions were designed to maintain the exterior envelope of the space.

Leaving the interior empty—or rather, filled with only nature—is a powerful narrative gesture that falls under the poetic approach. During the years of disinvestment, when the neighborhood was weighted down by the perception of blight, neighbors began caretaking, beautifying spaces with paint, plants, and pieces of exterior furniture. Working through discouragement and a feeling of disempowerment as the neighborhood emptied out,[17] neighbors did what they could. And thirty plus years later, one of the results of this caretaking and collaboration is the Granby Winter Garden. "It just is such a large-scale symbol of the planting that we've done and how long the impact of what we've done will last. And it's just beautiful," exclaims one resident.[18]

"It's a large-scale symbol of the planting that we've done."
—Granby resident

This is the vital narrative thread in Granby. Beauty is not an object—a set of Victorian tchotchkes or the muted ceramics for sale at the Granby Workshop. Beauty, as nineteenth-century preservation advocate William Morris

Queen Victoria's sitting room at Windsor Castle, circa 1862. (© Royal Collection Enterprises Limited 2024 | Royal Collection Trust.

The finished interior of one of the Victorian-era terraced homes, including the Granby Rock fireplace surround, 2017. (10 Houses on Cairns Street by Assemble Studio and the Granby Four Streets CLT. Granby Workshop. Photo by Lewis Jones)

Several of the completed terraced homes, circa 2017. (Gary Calton)

surely recognized, is in the making. Granby residents continue the making, seeding, growing, pruning, and caretaking that has characterized the neighborhood for years.

The Granby Four community's restoration of ten houses on Cairns Street, the creation of the Granby Ceramic Workshop, and the Granby Winter Garden are cooperative efforts that build on incremental actions. Funding for the Winter Garden was amassed from at least ten foundations and trusts.[19] Major funders require a track record and a glimpse of the big picture to risk involvement with a project. Thus the Winter Garden and ongoing projects in the neighborhood are predicated on earlier accomplishments.

These projects in Granby—ten houses on Cairns Street and the Granby Winter Garden—made use of resources internal to the community, such as creativity and caretaking, while counteracting the narrative of uselessness often attached to disinvested places. Elsewhere in the world, we can see a similar theme in the art of Tyree Guyton in Detroit, whose colorful dots across houses on Heidelberg Street (described in Chapter 5) could be seen as a protest of the demolition labels that marked vacant homes across the city. Similarly, one of Granby's residents noted that the city council's sign "nothing of value" was not only a painful label for the community but an agent of further devaluation.

Actions similar to those taken in Granby Four can be seen in partial or incremental restorations such as the Denny Row townhouses in the United States (described in Chapter 6) and priority repairs such as the structural steel brace holding up a ruined wall at Chantry Kilve (described in Chapter 4). The Granby Winter Garden is similar to other creative and larger-scale ideas for how greenspace and cultivation can work not only in vacant lots but also in vacant buildings, such as the Plant Concert project (profiled in Chapter 6), where plants become citizen-participants.

Granby and Cairns streets, 2019. (Audrey Walker Images/Alamy Stock Photo)

Sustainability is not only about building reuse or ecological interventions, such as reinhabiting a vacant interior with plant life. It's also about tapping into the regenerative capacity of the community, the ongoing economic and creative germination from initiatives such as the Granby Workshop and the monthly market featuring homemade, local, and second-hand goods. Incrementally building community economic health, maintaining housing affordability through rental and sale price covenants, celebrating creativity through workshops and markets, and honoring the residents' faithful contributions to the community continue to fuel Granby's momentum along the timeline of its restoration.

Rick Lowe, *Project Row Houses: Biggers and Beuys*, 2021. Acrylic and paper collage on canvas, 96 × 72 in. (243.8 × 182.9 cm). This collage, reminiscent of a street grid, honors two artists whose work were pillars for Project Row Houses. (© Rick Lowe Studio. Photo by Rob McKeever. Courtesy Gagosian)

Chapter 10

Social Sculpture

Houston: Project Row Houses and ModPod

Location: Houston, Texas, USA (Third Ward)
Featured time period: 1990–2015

It was a fall day in 1990 in Houston, Texas, and the air still smelled a bit like new beginnings and sharpened pencils. Artist Rick Lowe had invited a group of high school students for a conversation about his work at his studio in an industrial warehouse.

Lowe had just completed a protest exhibit about police brutality that included life-sized figural cutouts of victims of violence. The cutout figures and other billboard-sized paintings were arranged around Lowe's studio. He explained the sociopolitical nature of his work, his collaborations with social justice groups, and his personal motivations for addressing subjects such as police brutality and poverty.

A curious young man who had been very engaged in the presentation raised his hand.

"You know, Mr. Lowe, your paintings and sculptures show what happens in our communities," he began. "But we don't need that."

"We don't need people telling us what the issues are. We need solutions. If you're an artist and you're creative, why can't you create a solution?"[1]

"That," says Lowe, reflecting on the student's question over a decade later, "was the defining moment that pushed me out of the studio."[2] The student's challenge was an opening—like a hole blown through the side of the studio—through which Lowe began to look at the city and communities around him in a new way.

Houston's Third Ward, a traditionally African American and working-class neighborhood, contained many one-story wood frame houses colloquially called shotgun houses. These homes, built in the late nineteenth and early twentieth centuries, were only one room wide, with rooms sequenced front to back.[3] The house type had fallen out of favor, and many were abandoned.

Lowe says of the shotgun house, "If the shotgun house historically means anything in a community context, it's that it has no value. Seeing this kind of housing back in the early 90s and being part of a community group that was trying to deal with the bad, negative things in the community: this was the kind of thing they were saying we need to get rid of."[4]

Lowe credits one of his mentors, fellow Houston artist Dr. John Biggers, with calling his attention to the dignity and social support that the shotgun typology offered to prior generations. Biggers began to recontextualize the housing type for Lowe, pointing out that the single-file arrangement of the rooms reflected roots in the Caribbean house forms of enslaved Africans.[5] He described how the homes had served as a social safety net for the community.[6]

Biggers's painting *Four Seasons* is a celebration of the shotgun house and of the community that it shaped. In this painting, the architecture of serial row houses is featured as the backdrop or structure for community. The house fronts are portrait-like, appearing similar at a distance but revealing modifications and the individuality of the occupants on closer view. Explains a Project Row Houses (PRH) publication, "To Dr. Biggers, shotgun houses represented not just engineering prowess, but also the ingenuity required to build a community in an often-hostile climate—weather or otherwise. The repeating geometry of the row house in Biggers' artworks have become the Rosetta stone for the architectural vernacular of Third Ward. They are the building blocks of creative placekeeping of the African diaspora in the American South."[7]

Shifting the perception of this overlooked housing type became the focus of the work of Lowe and six other artists in Houston: James Bettison,

Four Seasons, 65/120, 1990, by John Biggers (1924–2001), colored lithograph. (© 2024 John T. Biggers Estate. Licensed by VAGA at Artists Rights Society [ARS], NY, Estate Represented by Michael Rosenfeld. Gibbes Museum of Art)

Bert Long Jr., Jesse Lott, Floyd Newsum, Bert Samples, and George Smith. Through this metaphorical hole in the studio wall, the group saw the possibilities in how, as they renovated the abandoned shotgun houses, their convictions about the social role of art could come to life together in a community. It was a new art project: Project Row Houses. In the decades since its inception, PRH has grown to encompass six blocks and fifty properties, with a programmatic focus on public art, arts education, affordable housing, and supporting young mothers.

PRH was officially incorporated as a nonprofit in 1993, establishing a vehicle for funding for the shotgun houses that had captured the artists' imagination. A $25,000 Art in Public Places grant from the National Endowment for the Arts was the seed that facilitated a lease–purchase agreement on the houses on a block and a half, which had been platted as one property. The group reached out to cultural and community institutions to "adopt" one house each, either by financing a house or by showing up to do the work. The vision was to provide space for visiting and local artists to live, work, and

The row houses before renovation, circa early 1990s. (Photo by Sheryl Tucker Vasquez. Courtesy of Project Row Houses)

The row houses in 2015. (Photo by Peter Molik. Courtesy of Project Row Houses)

Participants in a workshop with one of the Project Row Houses shotgun houses as a backdrop, 1997. (Photo courtesy Project Row Houses)

engage with the community. By 1994, ten shotgun houses had been renovated as Art Houses. Later, PRH focused on renovating other shotgun houses in the neighborhood as homes for single mothers. In total, twenty-two shotgun houses were renovated as part of the project.

The focus was on the use value of the shotgun houses as a creative generator. They have become experimental studio space, community gathering space, and living space for new and legacy residents. Lowe explains that PRH's goal was not to create empty containers or structures that looked back to a specific moment in time. "It is not our intent to create a museum to a culture that once was, to preserve homes as shells and reminders of a storied past. Project Row Houses succeeds as a social sculpture when Black art, culture, and community are protected, promoted, elevated, and celebrated in

Young Mothers Program activities with the Project Row Houses shotgun houses as backdrop, 1997. (Photo courtesy Project Row Houses)

> *"There's a balance between preservation and development by centering creativity and engagement at the fulcrum."*
> *—Clare Cumberlidge and Lucy Musgrave*

new and vibrant ways that honor the past but build a dynamic, diverse, and unique future."[8] Authors Clare Cumberlidge and Lucy Musgrave observe that PRH finds a balance "between preservation and development by centering creativity and engagement at the fulcrum."[9]

The renovation of the PRH shotgun houses primarily retains their original exterior aesthetic, in contrast to the more experimental approach of Theaster Gates for the Archive House on Dorchester in Chicago. As Lowe tells it, Sheryl Tucker de Vazquez was "the architect in the circle who we were leaning on a lot"[10] as the group pulled repair permits for the work. Architect Stennis Lenoir also helped inspire progress by contextualizing the ongoing repair and restoration work within John Biggers's notion of the mythological proportions of the shotgun house.

Chapter 2 introduced the idea of social sculpture as described by artist Joseph Beuys. Biggers (1924–2001) and Beuys (1921–1986), two roughly

The exhibit Third Ward Archive by artist Tracy Hicks, 1996. (Photo courtesy Project Row Houses)

The jars in the Third Ward Archive exhibit contained historic images and photographs taken by residents with disposable cameras, 1996. (Photo courtesy Project Row Houses)

contemporaneous artists from different parts of the world, became philosophical pillars for PRH. Beuys's notion of social sculpture taking shape from artistic and human capital is demonstrated in not only how the shotgun houses were renovated but also how the neighborhood began to transform as PRH brought on more partners.

In the late 1990s, PRH began a collaboration with the nearby Rice University School of Architecture that was facilitated by professors Daniel (Danny) Samuels and Nonya Grenader through the Rice Building Workshop, located on the PRH campus. This partnership, which has continued for decades, resulted in research and numerous built projects such as the ZeRo house, which runs on solar energy, and the use of consolidated cores in renovation and new construction.

A consolidated core groups mechanical, plumbing, and electrical services together in one area of the building. It can reduce renovation costs, as upgrading the mechanical, electrical, and plumbing systems is one of the greater logistical challenges and thus expenses in older buildings. In the 2010s, three

Rice architecture graduate students, Andrew Daley, Peter Muessig, and Jason Fleming, joined the research and experimentation on consolidated cores. The students wanted to prefabricate a core for a residence.

Together with PRH, the students selected the Freedmen's Town House as a prototype to receive the prefabricated core. The Freedmen's Town House, also called the Bastrop House, is a shotgun-style house originally built in the adjacent Fourth Ward around the turn of the twentieth century. The house and nine adjacent homes were some of the last remaining structures that characterized the historic district, an area where formerly enslaved people settled with their families.[11] The neighborhood was under extreme pressure from development, and as discussed in the profile on moving structures in Chapter 4, this is the primary reason that historic resources are relocated. The Freedmen's Town House was moved to a lot on Bastrop Street in the PRH neighborhood and readied for renovation.

At the Rice Building Workshop, the graduate students built a prototype of a core unit they called the ModPod. The 8.5- × 12-foot unit contained a bathroom, galley kitchen, and mechanical closet. The ModPod was installed into the Freedman's Town House in one day, with readily available construction equipment. Reduced on-site construction time minimizes vandalism and theft opportunities. Consolidated cores such as the ModPod offer the benefits of energy and technology upgrades with minimal intervention to an existing structure.

The concept of the consolidated core is a great example of engaging incrementally at the building scale. Like the shell strategy profiled in Denny

Photo collage of the ModPod unit being inserted into the Freemen's Town House. (Image produced by Andrew Daley, Jason Fleming, and Peter Muessig)

Row in Chapter 6, consolidated cores address some of the most technically challenging, labor-intensive aspects of the work in one package. This frees the owner or occupant to complete the remainder of the work incrementally as funds and know-how are available, offering the latitude of a detached timeline.

A key action of PRH from the beginning has been artistic activism through poetic, narrative art projects. One of the first exhibits in the neighborhood, organized by Jesse Lott and Rick Lowe, was called *Drive-By*. The exhibit and its name capitalized on the increased traffic driving by to see what was going on with the row houses while critically evoking the drive-by shootings that were taking place in the neighborhood in the 1990s.[12] Lott and Lowe invited artists to use the plywood as their canvas, using it to board up the doors and windows of the row houses before they were renovated.

Drive-By exhibit prep at Project Row Houses, 1993. (Photo by Israel McCloud. Courtesy of Project Row Houses)

Around the world and across diverse building types, there's a history of using the side of buildings as billboards or canvases, whether for monetary, political, or artistic purposes. In the nineteenth and early twentieth century, farmers allowed advertisements on the sides of their barns as a way of getting the barn painted for free. Warehouse sides have become movie screens. Cathedral fronts have become the backdrop for elaborate light shows. In 2023, climate activists draped the British prime minister's manor house in

Wood façades as billboards are a longstanding vernacular tradition in the United States. This photo depicts Andrea Bower's 2010 installation *Hope in Hindsight* at Project Row Houses. (Courtesy of Project Row Houses. Photo by Eric Hester)

A freshly painted (or repainted) Mail Pouch Tobacco sign on a barn in rural Jackson County, West Virginia, 2015. (Library of Congress, Prints & Photographs Division, photograph by Carol M. Highsmith [LC-DIG-highsm-31890])

black to protest his stance on oil and gas reserves.[13] PRH continues to offer the Art Houses as a canvas.

It's a fascinating inversion of Biggers's original painting, which contained the shotgun houses on a canvas. As a 2006 *New York Times* article by Michael Kimmelman points out, at PRH the shotgun houses have become the canvas, and the neighborhood and its residents are an artwork of an entirely different scale.[14]

At PRH, the social sculpture or engagement process was built on shifting the value of the shotgun house, pushing against a prevailing narrative to connect the story of the homes to a broader historical narrative. Over time, house-scaled efforts broadened to physically larger and financially more complex projects such as the renovation of the Eldorado Ballroom, a historical music venue that continues its cultural role in the community. "Finding value in undervalued objects, places, and people flows organically from PRH's history of artistic practice and its commitment to viewing the project as more of a creative act than a producer of created objects, as a living social sculpture rather than an ideal physical environment,"[15] writes Black studies scholar George Lipsitz in a twenty-fifth anniversary publication celebrating PRH.

The shotgun house has been called the "basic ingredient" of PRH's revitalization efforts.[16] This ingredient, in both poetic and very pragmatic ways, has served a transformative purpose in the PRH community and in the lives of many who have passed through and interacted with the community. Says Assata-Nicole Richards, who was a Young Mothers Program participant in the 1990s, "I now teach others what I learned from the artists and through my own transformation, which is the profound truth that we all possess the capacity to sculpt ourselves and the world arounds us to better serve us individually and collectively."[17]

Project Row Houses neighborhood entrance sign. (Photo by Caesandra Seawell)

Candy Chang's public installation *Looking for Love Again*, 2011. (Candy Chang)

Conclusion

"As an artist or an architect, I have the opportunity to address wrongs and try to correct them."

—Samuel Mockbee, samuelmockbee.net

In the mid-1990s, I was living in Chicago and working at a small firm on urban design and affordable housing projects. My colleague Patrick and I went to hear then–relatively unknown architect Samuel Mockbee speak at the Graham Foundation. I haven't been able to locate any transcripts of this lecture, but this is how I remember it.

We filed into the close, darkened room and settled into our seats. One by one, his eloquent murals and humane constructions filled the screen, and his rough voice penetrated the space. But, as it turns out, the lecture wasn't about Mockbee and his work at all. The lecture was about the audience (mostly architects), we of the city, we of the ivory tower. We were looking aside. We were narcissistically focused. We were not doing enough to address poverty. My conscience was piqued.

It was certainly one of the most unusual architecture lectures I had ever attended. It had more the character of an old-fashioned tent revival.

The Gospel Train, 1929, by John Steuart Curry (1897–1946), oil painting. (Syracuse University Art Museum, New York, USA/Bridgeman Images)

Patrick and I put on our coats and began our ten-block walk to the Sedgwick El station. My soul knew that Mockbee was right, but my pride and my practicality welled up, and all of my responses came out as indignation, coming from my mouth in frosty word ribbons sent out to the night sky.

"What does he want us to do?"

"This is Chicago, not rural Alabama."

"We just can't start building a shelter out of abandoned materials."

"We've got building codes, zoning regulations, funding restrictions to consider."

As a young architectural intern, freshly minted from the university, I could not reconcile the urgency of the need with the layers of civic structure I was encountering—with the process that we as a society had developed to make buildings safer and to better our collective environment. I couldn't integrate the two. Trying to do so only made me feel impotent, angry.

I also didn't have the maturity at that time to understand that his lecture wasn't really a chastisement but an invitation to engage. Our engagement, as I believe Mockbee was trying to point out, requires not only compassion but courage, and a deep and sometimes critical creativity.

And engagement is messy. It can be easily second-guessed. As a perfectionist, I struggle with all the decisions that difficult projects engender and regret for the mistakes that I've surely made along the way. Our discomfort with the messy is part and parcel with the process—a process that's sometimes an unsettling meander through gray areas. Architect Dana Cuff referred to it as an "uneasy agonism [that] is fundamental to ethical practices of design."[1]

Indeed, this unsettling meander—sometimes difficult, sometimes energizing, sometimes sorrowful, and sometimes startlingly beautiful—*is* the work. In an insightful book about the process of editing his own life for a movie script, author Donald Miller says, "The point of a story is never about the ending, remember. It's about your character getting molded in the hard work of the middle."[2]

I think about my friend Flora. She and my husband climbed through the front window of a grand house in Detroit's Boston Edison neighborhood in the early 2000s. In the twilight that evening, around the remains of a campfire someone had built in the middle of the living room, she dreamed of bringing that home back to life. She dedicated the next ten years of her life and income to it. And when she had to move on, she found she could no longer drive past that house where the original wood windows that she had painstakingly restored had later been ripped out for vinyl replacements.

Flora wrote me a beautiful letter about the lessons she learned restoring that house and how the process changed her. But she was not the only one molded by the work of the middle, to use Miller's phrase. There's a conservation of energy in the universe, and I believe that the energy Flora put into that house—the finances, the sweat and tears, the worry and care along with the joy and delight—couldn't have produced only a change in her own character. Those years for the house in Boston Edison, and Flora's participation in them, helped mold the character of the neighborhood.

Stewart Brand's 1994 book *How Buildings Learn* explained that buildings learn by adapting to and being adapted by the humans who use them. The concept holds true on a broader scale. Neighborhoods and communities are also evidence of our involvement with them. Their morphology is a record of our values as individuals and as a society, reflecting our attempts to erase or control or our willingness and courage to edit and adapt.

Artist Candy Chang's community project *Looking for Love Again* called attention to an abandoned residential high-rise in Fairbanks, Alaska. In addition to the four-story banner with the project name at the top of the building, the interactive project included chalkboards along the sidewalk and a website that invited people to record their reflections on how this building had been a part of their lives and their hopes for its future. The dating app tagline is an anthropomorphic approach, encouraging consideration of how the building could be brought back into relationship with the community.

In Chicago, Houston, Liverpool, and rural Virginia, we've seen how incremental actions on existing buildings over time can build momentum and attract investment for larger-scope projects. In the case of Menokin, the Stony Island Arts Bank, and the Eldorado Ballroom, the momentum has contributed to the preservation of a historic structure. But these preservation successes are not the apex of the story. House-scaled projects such as the Remembrance Structure, the Dorchester Projects, 10 Houses on Cairns, and Project Row Houses have been a fertile middle ground that has invited others in, broadened participation, and increased creative energy around them.

Chalkboard memories in Candy Chang's public installation *Looking for Love Again*, 2011. (Candy Chang)

This book features projects that demonstrate how existing buildings and their sites, with necessary safety modifications or code-required upgrades, can become temporary or permanent shelters. They can be part of an environmental remediation or a food-growing enterprise. They can teach skills and become the locus of ongoing participation and renewal. All of these uses have practical benefits when a building and site are brought back in relationship with community.

But even the featured projects that don't have a practical benefit—interventions with existing buildings that are perhaps better described as art than architecture—have importance to all of us. These buildings tell stories about our collective past and provide perspective on critical issues. They can prompt thoughtful reflection or conversation. Buildings with interesting interventions help us—and especially our children—to ask why. We may not have all the answers. I certainly didn't at twenty, and I don't now. But they help us enter into the questions.

Buildings continue to be disproportionately removed from disinvested communities and are slowly disappearing from demolition by neglect. A third of the case studies featured in this book (the priority projects) are about individuals and communities just trying to save a building for the future. Some of the case studies feature buildings that are already gone, such as the Mullanphy building. Some of the projects were temporary, such as Les Grands Voisins, or are partially finished, like Bánffy Castle. Most of the projects featured in this book will continue to morph and change.

Distressed buildings need all kinds of people—the pragmatic, the brave, the visionary, the technical—to weave a way through financing and codes, through ethical and environmental considerations. The projects in this book—and many others around the globe—have been leading the way for years, most with very little fanfare.

This conclusion is a closing that is really an opening. Whether you are a community resident or activist, architect or artist, this book is an invitation to engage with each other and with our buildings. It's about gathering courage to act, to participate, to mend. It's a call to continue to thoughtfully adapt our preservation standards to be more porous, to adjust our ways of working to serve the broader health, safety, and wellness of all society, and to advocate for the reuse of existing buildings.

Demolition is not the only destiny for vacant, abandoned, and distressed buildings. Preserving with purpose can benefit communities, society, and our environment, recalibrating our course, incrementally, toward the greater good.

Notes

PREFACE

1. John George, founder of Detroit Blight Busters, provided context for how the Blight Mobile catalyzed efforts across the city for Angel's Night in the late 1990s, a citizen patrol to combat arson in the days leading up to Halloween. Author interview with John George, March 2024.
2. Mari Gallagher, "Examining the Impact of Food Deserts on Public Health in Detroit," Mari Gallagher Research & Consulting Group, 2007. In 2013, the US Department of Agriculture stopped using the term "food desert," replacing it with the descriptor "low income and low access."
3. Michigan metal theft tripled between 2011 and 2012 according to state police reports, as cited in Jonathan Oosting, "Michigan Seeks to Crack Down on Metal Theft with New Law Signed by Gov. Rick Snyder," Mlive.com, April 10, 2014, https://www.mlive.com/lansing-news/2014/04/michigan_looks_to_crack_down_o.html.
4. Author interview with John George, March 2024.
5. Lewis Carroll, *Alice's Adventures in Wonderland* (Macmillan, 1865).

INTRODUCTION

1. Jia Lok Pratt and Emmanuel Pratt, "Designing for Public Trust: From Bounded Rationality to Unbounded Possibilities," *Harvard Design Magazine* 49 (2022): 128.

2. Anthony Balas, "Re-Generation and Re-Storying with the Sweet Water Foundation," *The Mellon Foundation*, October 4, 2022, https://www.mellon.org/grant-story/re-generation-and-re-storying-with-sweet-water-foundation.
3. Johnny Miller, "Roads to Nowhere: How Infrastructure Built on American Inequality," *The Guardian*, February 21, 2018, https://www.theguardian.com/cities/2018/feb/21/roads-nowhere-infrastructure-american-inequality.
4. Richard Moe in National Trust for Historic Preservation, *Rebuilding Community: A Best Practices Toolkit for Historic Preservation and Redevelopment* (National Trust Publication, 2002).
5. "A community's decision to foster the sustainable and appropriate reuse of its abandoned and underutilized properties reflects faith in the future of the city and its neighborhoods. This faith is not always present. In many distressed cities, the pervasive lack of hope among the citizens and their leaders has deep roots." Alan Mallach, *Bringing Buildings Back: From Abandoned Properties to Community Assets* (The National Housing Institute, 2010), 192.

   Mindy Thompson Fullilove's book *Root Shock* explores the ongoing sociological effects of urban renewal and demolition. Mindy Thompson Fullilove, *Root Shock: How Tearing Up City Neighborhoods Hurts America, and What We Can Do About It* (Random House, 2004).
6. Jason Hackworth, "Demolition as Urban Policy in the American Rust Belt," *Environment and Planning A*, 48(11) (2016): 2201–2222, 2215.
7. Center for Community Progress, "Systemic Vacancy: What Is a Vacant, Abandoned, or Deteriorated Property?," https://communityprogress.org/resources/vacancy/.
8. Center for Community Progress, "Explaining the Cycle of Systemic Vacancy." August 24, 2023, https://communityprogress.org/blog/explaining-systemic-vacancy/#:~:text=The%20cycle%20of%20systemic%20vacancy%20can%20be%20broken%20down%20into,increased%20vacancy%20on%20the%20community.
9. Balas, "Re-Generation and Re-Storying."
10. The Sweet Water Foundation, "Introducing the Civic Arts Church 2021 | Redefining Historic Preservation at The Commonwealth," https://www.sweetwaterfoundation.com/civic-arts-church.
11. Ibid.

12. Beth Brant, "Some Buildings Are Special. Some Are Not. The Majority of Them Should Be Reused," AIA Dallas *Columns* 1, no 4 (Fall 2024), https://www.aiadallas.org/columns/.
13. Alan Mallach, *The Divided City: Poverty and Prosperity in Urban America* (Island Press, 2018), 115.
14. Author John Stubbs notes that the term *historic preservation* is likely to endure in the United States, although the use of the term *conservation* is becoming more universally prevalent. John Stubbs, *Time Honored: A Global View of Architectural Conservation* (John Wiley and Sons, 2009), 24, 30.
15. Mark Byrnes, "When Do Buildings Deserve a Second Chance?," *Bloomberg City Lab*, September 1, 2023, https://www.bloomberg.com/news/features/2023-09-01/for-architect-deborah-berke-there-s-magic-in-adaptive-reuse.
16. Ayn Rand, *The Fountainhead* (Bobbs Merrill, 1943). Howard Roark is the architect-protagonist in Rand's novel.

CHAPTER 1

1. Kim Kozlowski, "Detroit's 70 Year Population Decline Continues; Duggan Says City was Undercounted," *The Detroit News*, August 12, 2021, https://www.detroitnews.com/story/news/local/detroit-city/2021/08/12/census-detroit-population-decline-u-s-census-bureau/5567639001/.
2. In 2008, a graphic produced by Professor Dan Pitera and the University of Detroit Mercy went viral by skillfully depicting the scale of Detroit's shrinking population and, in corollary, its resources, without a reduction in the demands of its infrastructure. John Gallagher, "Detroit: Land of Opportunity: Acres of Barren Blocks Offer Chance to Reinvent City," *Detroit Free Press*, December 15, 2008.
3. According to the Vacant Properties Research Network, "Few studies of blighted properties address the production of blight. But when the subject is addressed, the conclusion is unanimous: blighted land is not a problem that cities inherited from the past, but an active creation of contemporary urban policies and a series of non-economic forces. . . . Vacancy and abandonment, in other words, are the outcome of a particular set of structural forces, institutional mechanisms, and powerful decisions by individuals." Vacant Properties Research Network for Keep America Beautiful, "Charting the Multiple Meanings of Blight: A National Literature Review on Addressing the Community Impacts of Blighted

Properties. Final Report," May 19, 2015, 11, http://communitylaw.org/wp-content/uploads/2016/03/Charting-the-Multiple-Meanings-of-Blight-FINAL-2015-05-19.pdf.

4. Joseph Schilling and Jimena Pinzón, "The Basics of Blight: Recent Research on Its Drivers, Impacts, and Interventions," *VPRN Research and Policy Brief* 2 (2016): 11.
5. Andrew Hurley, "Making Preservation Work for Struggling Communities: A Plea to Loosen National Historic District Guidelines," in Max Page and Marla R. Miller, *Bending the Future: 50 Ideas for the Next 50 Years of Historic Preservation in the United States* (University of Massachusetts Press, 2016).
6. Center for Community Progress, "The Scale and Cost of Blight in Michigan," June 2022, https://communityprogress.org/wp-content/uploads/2022/06/One-pager_Michigan-Blight-v2.pdf.
7. Mark Binelli, "How Detroit Became the World Capital of Staring at Abandoned Old Buildings," *New York Times Magazine,* November 9, 2012, https://www.nytimes.com/2012/11/11/magazine/how-detroit-became-the-world-capital-of-staring-at-abandoned-old-buildings.html.
8. In 2014, the tap also turned off on the Detroit water system for 30,000 households whose bills were past due. The UN declared the disconnection a violation of human rights. See UN Press Release on Detroit water disconnections, June 25, 2014, https://www.ohchr.org/en/press-releases/2014/06/detroit-disconnecting-water-people-who-cannot-pay-affront-human-rights-say#:~:text=The%20Detroit%20Water%20and%20Sewerage,around%203%2C000%20customers%20per%20week.
9. Center for Community Progress, "Explaining the Cycle of Systemic Vacancy," August 24, 2023, https://communityprogress.org/blog/explaining-systemic-vacancy/.
10. Center for Community Progress, "How Vacant and Abandoned Buildings Affect the Community," April 10, 2024, https://communityprogress.org/blog/how-vacant-abandoned-buildings-affect-community/.

    In his book *Bringing Buildings Back*, planner Alan Mallach says, "When abandoned properties constitute as little as 3 to 5 percent of the buildings in a neighborhood, abandonment may begin to feed on itself as property owners see the abandoned properties in their midst as harbingers of further neighborhood decline." Alan Mallach, *Bringing Buildings Back: From Abandoned Properties to Community Assets* (National Housing Institute, 2010), 9.

11. Detroit Blight Removal Task Force, "Every Neighborhood Has a Future . . . and It Doesn't Include Blight," *Detroit Blight Removal Task Force Plan*, May 27, 2014, https://www.documentcloud.org/documents/1173946-detroit-blight-removal-task-force-plan-may-2014.html?embed=true&responsive=false&sidebar=true; also accessible through https://www.nytimes.com/interactive/2014/05/27/us/detroit-blight.html.
12. Christine Ferretti, "Last Detroit House Demolished in $265M Blight Removal Effort," *The Detroit News*, August 14, 2020, https://www.detroitnews.com/story/news/local/detroit-city/2020/08/14/last-detroit-house-demolished-blight-removal/3349213001/.
13. Detroit Future City, "139 Square Miles," Inland Press, 2017, p. 69, https://detroitfuturecity.com/wp-content/uploads/2017/11/DFC_139-SQ-Mile_Report.pdf.
14. University of Michigan, "Detroit Metro Areas Communities Study," *Issue Brief: Blight in Detroit*, Spring 2020, https://detroitsurvey.umich.edu/wp-content/uploads/2021/02/Blight-Report-7-21-2020.pdf.
15. Michael Roman-John Koscielniak's 2020 dissertation explored the socioeconomic forces around blight removal in Detroit, framing it in terms of a production of decline. "This is the circulation of money, supplies, and materials, but it is also the circulation of power and control over the fortunes of Detroit neighborhoods. Demolition is not a local *program*; it [is] a regional process and an achievement by power and capital." Michael Roman-John Koscielniak, "Ground Forces: Dirt, Demolition, and the Geography of Decline in Detroit, Michigan," PhD diss. (University of Michigan, 2020), 316.
16. Erwin deLeon and Joseph Schilling, "Research Report: Urban Blight and Public Health Addressing the Impact of Substandard Housing, Abandoned Buildings, and Vacant Lots," *The Urban Institute*, April 11, 2017, https://www.urban.org/research/publication/urban-blight-and-public-health.
17. C. Bezold, S. J. Bauer, J. P. Buckley, S. Batterman, H. Haroon, and L. Fink, "Demolition Activity and Elevated Blood Lead Levels Among Children in Detroit, Michigan, 2014–2018," *International Journal of Environmental Research and Public Health* 17, no. 17 (August 19, 2020): 6018, doi:10.3390/ijerph17176018.
18. Center for Community Progress, "The Problem with Calling Neighborhoods with Vacant Properties Blighted," March 30, 2023, https://communityprogress.org/blog/what-is-blight/.

19. In his book *The Divided City*, planner Alan Mallach says, "Indeed, the idea one hears that urban demolition is a stalking horse for future gentrification is yet another urban myth; in reality, it more often creates a moonscape of vacant land that all but guarantees gentrification will *not* take place." Alan Mallach, *The Divided City: Poverty and Prosperity in Urban America* (Island Press, 2018), 111.

    In their article "Planning for Better, Smaller Places After Population Loss: Lessons from Youngstown and Flint," authors Dewar, Kelly, and Morrison offer lessons for planners, several of which coincide with discussions in this book. They also propose acting expeditiously to get rid of liabilities, in which they discuss and advocate demolition. I would caveat that although some demolition is needed and reasonable, an empty building does not only represent a liability in the context of a disinvested community. In this book, I make the case for careful consideration of options (*quick* is often in conflict with *strategic*) in view of a building's potential in the near and longer term. See Margaret Dewar and June Manning Thomas (eds.), *The City After Abandonment* (University of Pennsylvania Press, 2013).
20. Sidney K. Robinson, "The Picturesque: Sinister Dishevelment," in Marco Diani and Catherine Ingraham (eds.), *Restructuring Architectural Theory* (Rizzoli, 1988), 74–79.
21. "If you look superficially this is exploitation. If you take the time and look more profoundly, this is connection," said Ryan Mendoza in "Why I Took a Family's House from Detroit to Rotterdam," *The Guardian*, February 24, 2016, https://www.theguardian.com/housing-network/2016/feb/24/white-man-black-family-home-detroit-rotterdam.
22. Mark Stryker, "Artist Takes Abandoned Detroit Home, Leaves Mess Behind," *The Detroit Free Press*, March 25, 2016.
23. Catherine Slessor, "Reading the Ruins," *The Architectural Review*, December 21, 2017, https://www.architectural-review.com/essays/reading-the-ruins/10026503.article.
24. Rod Meloni, "Neighbors, city upset after artist strips Detroit home, leaves blight behind," WDIV Detroit, March 25, 5016, https://www.clickondetroit.com/news/2016/03/25/neighbors-city-upset-after-artist-strips-detroit-home-leaves-blight-behind/.
25. Drew Philp, *A $500 House in Detroit: Rebuilding an Abandoned Home and an American City* (Scribner, 2017), 105.
26. Estate of Charles McGee webpage, Library Street Collective, https://lscgallery.com/charles-mcgee-estate.

27. Patrice Frey, "Why Historic Preservation Needs a New Approach," *Bloomberg City Lab Perspective*, February 8, 2019, https://www.bloomberg.com/news/articles/2019-02-08/why-historic-preservation-needs-a-new-approach.
28. Ibid.
29. Friends of Notre-Dame de Paris, "Spire of Notre-Dame de Paris to Be Rebuilt According to 19th Century Design," undated, https://www.friendsofnotredamedeparis.org/spire-notre-dame-paris-fire/.
30. Eugene-Emmanuel Viollet-le-Duc, *Dictionnaire Raisonné de l'Architecture Française*, paraphrase by author, https://www.cosa-paris.com/restauration-eugene-emmanuel-viollet-le-duc/?lang=en.
31. David Spurr, "Figures of Ruin and Restoration: Ruskin and Viollet-le-Duc," *Architecture and Modern Literature* (University of Michigan Press, 2012).
32. John Ruskin, *The Seven Lamps of Architecture* (Smith, Elder, and Company, 1849).
33. Preservation professor Max Page points out that a focus on the architectural significance of the building misses the importance of storytelling. "In their focus on architectural significance, American preservationists have done little in the way of interpretation—explaining the significance of the site. . . . But as compelling as places can be to our eyes and hearts, they do not tell their stories on their own. Places do not speak; we must speak for them." Max Page, *Why Preservation Matters* (Yale University Press, 2016), 53.
34. Stephanie Meeks, *The Past and Future City: How Historic Preservation Is Reviving America's Communities* (Island Press, 2016), 185.
35. A discussion with Susan Ross, an architect and academic who works in sustainable heritage planning and conservation, inspired this question. Ross notes that considering only selected architectural elements as having heritage value helps to define the rest as potential waste or discards. Susan M. Ross, "Re-Evaluating Heritage Waste: Sustaining Material Values Through Deconstruction and Reuse," *The Historic Environment: Policy & Practice* 11, no. 2–3 (2020): 382–408.
36. Frey's article also underscores the need to be flexible on some of the "preservation standards sometimes held sacrosanct," because, concludes Frey later in her article, "in some instances, compromise is appropriate in order to accommodate other important social goods and economic realities." Frey, "Why Historic Preservation Needs a New Approach."

    David Brown, in his article "A Preservation Movement for All Americans," also wonders whether preservationists are "too attached to tools designed to fight the last war." David Brown, "A Preservation Movement for All Americans," in Max Page and Marla R. Miller, *Bending the Future: 50 Ideas for the Next 50 Years of Historic Preservation in the United States* (University of Massachusetts Press, 2016).

37. National Historic Designation Advisory Committee, "Recommendations for Improving the Recognition of Historic Properties of Importance to All Americans: Executive Summary," National Conference of State Historic Preservation Officers, April 2023, https://ncshpo.org/wp-content/uploads/2023/04/NHDAC-Executive-Summary.pdf.
38. Robert C. Burns, posted in AIA Historic Resources Committee discussion group, November 16, 2023. Used with permission.

CHAPTER 2

1. Eric Klinenberg, *Heat Wave: A Social Autopsy of Disaster in Chicago* (University of Chicago Press, 2002).
2. Eric Klinenberg, *Palaces for the People: How Social Infrastructure Can Help Fight Inequality, Polarization, and the Decline of Civic Life* (Penguin Random House, 2018), 5.
3. Ibid., 6.
4. Alan Mallach, *The Divided City: Poverty and Prosperity in Urban America* (Island Press, 2018), 111.
5. Architect Carl Elefante is credited with the phrase "The greenest building is . . . one that is already built." For commercial buildings, 35 percent of the expected lifetime carbon emission of the building has already been spent by the conclusion of the construction process. For residential buildings, this figure is over 50 percent. Royal Institution of Chartered Surveyors (RICS), "Whole Life Carbon Assessment for the Built Environment," November 2017, 3, https://www.rics.org/content/dam/ricsglobal/documents/standards/whole_life_carbon_assessment_for_the_built_environment_1st_edition_rics.pdf.
6. M. Desirée Alba-Rodríguez, Alejandro Martínez-Rocamora, Patricia González-Vallejo, Antonio Ferreira-Sánchez, and Madelyn Marrero, "Building Rehabilitation Versus Demolition and New Construction: Economic and Environmental Assessment," *Environmental Impact Assessment Review* 66 (2017): 115–26, https://doi.org/10.1016/j.eiar.2017.06.002.
7. Mike Jackson, "Embodied Energy and Historic Preservation: A Needed Re-Assessment," *APT Bulletin* 36, no. 4 (2005): 47–52, Table 4.

8. Thomas De Monchaux, "Promise: Variations on the Architecture of Transformational Change," in Deborah Berke and Thomas De Monchaux, *Transform: Promising Places, Second Chances, and the Architecture of Transformational Change*, ed. Arthi Krishnamoorthy (Monacelli Press, 2023).
9. Place Economics, "Twenty-Four Reasons Historic Preservation Is Good for Your Community," 2020, https://www.placeeconomics.com/wp-content/uploads/2020/01/City-Studies-WP-Online-Doc.pdf.
10. Alois Riegl, "The Modern Cult of Monuments: Its Character and Its Origin," 1903, as explained in John H. Stubbs, *Time Honored: A Global View of Architectural Conservation* (John Wiley and Sons, 2009), 38.
11. Erica Avrami, "Finding the Soul of Communities. An Interview with Claudia Guerra," in *Issues in Preservation Policy: Preservation and Social Inclusion* (Columbia Books on Architecture and the City, 2020).
12. Rosanne Haggerty, "Keeping Us Honest: What Our Buildings Tell Us About the Health of Our Communities," in Max Page and Marla R. Miller, *Bending the Future: 50 Ideas for the Next 50 Years of Historic Preservation in the United States* (University of Massachusetts Press, 2016).
13. Candy Chang website, Candychang.com/work/i-wish-this-was/.
14. Jessica Goad, Matt Lee-Ashley, and Farah Z. Ahmad, "Better Reflecting Our Country's Growing Diversity: Progress Has Been Made, but Work Remains for National Parks and Monuments," *Center for American Progress*, February 19, 2014, https://www.americanprogress.org/article/better-reflecting-our-countrys-growing-diversity/.
15. UNESCO, https://whc.unesco.org/en/list/stat/.
16. World Monument Watch, 2022, https://www.wmf.org/2022watch.
17. Ibid.
18. American Forest Management, "Recognizing Property Boundaries," November 2, 2017, https://www.americanforestmanagement.com/news/recognizing-property-boundaries.
19. Reimagining the Civic Commons, "A New Narrative for Disinvested Neighborhoods: Countering Stigma, Spurring New Models of Growth," *Medium*, December 20, 2023, https://medium.com/reimagining-the-civic-commons/a-new-narrative-for-disinvested-neighborhoods-d9fb16d444a9.
20. Robert Sampson, *Great American City: Chicago and the Enduring Neighborhood Effect* (University of Chicago Press, 2012), as cited in Daniel Hertz, "Let's Talk About Neighborhood Stigma," *City Observatory*, March 8, 2015, https://cityobservatory.org/lets-talk-about-neighborhood-stigma/.

21. Chris Harris, "After Generations of Disinvestment, Rural America Might Be the Most Innovative Place in the U.S.," *Ewing Marion Kauffman Foundation*. December 14, 2020, https://www.kauffman.org/currents/rural-america-most-innovative-place-in-united-states/.
22. Dolores Hayden, *The Power of Place: Urban Landscapes as Public History* (MIT Press, 1995), 46–7.
23. International Coalition of Sites of Conscience, https://www.sitesofconscience.org/about-us/about-us-2/.
24. Transcribed from "In the Glass with Menokin: The Remembrance Structure," video by the Menokin Foundation, https://www.menokin.org/remembrance-structure.
25. Clare Cumberlidge and Lucy Musgrave, *Design and Landscape for People: New Approaches for Renewal* (Thames and Hudson, 2007), 163–167.
26. David Brown, "A Preservation Movement for all Americans," in Max Page and Marla R. Miller, *Bending the Future: 50 Ideas for the Next 50 Years of Historic Preservation in the United States* (University of Massachusetts Press, 2016).
27. James Marston Fitch, *Historic Preservation: Curatorial Management of the Built World* (University of Virginia Press, 1982).
28. Two resources are Alan Mallach's *Bringing Buildings Back: From Abandoned Properties to Community Assets* (National Housing Institute, 2010); and the Center for Community Progress's "Context" pillar of Vacant Land Stewardship, https://communityprogress.org/resources/vacant-land/elements/.
29. Avrami, "Finding the Soul of Community."
30. Claudia Guerra, as quoted in Erica Avrami, "Finding the Soul of Community."
31. ExRotaprint, "What Is ExRotaprint?," https://www.exrotaprint.de/en/exrotaprint-ggmbh/.
32. Willemien van Duijn and Lieuwe Vos, *Freestyle 03. Abandoned Cities* (BNA Onderzoek, 2012), 65
33. Veronica Esposito, "'A Way to Build on Our Ancestral Legacy': Artists Reclaim a Major Center of Black Culture," *The Guardian*, February 1, 2024, https://www.theguardian.com/artanddesign/2024/feb/01/this-way-art-exhibit-houston-contemporary-arts-museum-freedmens-town.
34. Rosie Nguyen, "Bricks of Freedmen's Town Symbolizes Community's Legacy of Strength and Resilience," *ABC13.com*, June 15, 2023, https://abc13.com/freedmens-town-bricks-fourth-ward-andrews-street/13385784/.

35. Dr. Martin Luther King, Jr., *Where Do We Go from Here: Chaos or Community?* (Harper and Row, 1967).
36. Andrew Hurley, "Making Preservation Work for Struggling Communities: A Plea to Loosen National Historic District Guidelines," in Max Page and Marla R. Miller, *Bending the Future: 50 Ideas for the Next 50 Years of Historic Preservation in the United States* (University of Massachusetts Press, 2016).

CHAPTER 3

1. Author interview with Rick Lowe, December 2024.
2. Ibid.
3. C. L. Bohannon, "Radical Reimagination," in "Field Notes on Repair: 3," *Places Journal*, November 2024, https://placesjournal.org/article/field-notes-on-repair-3/#:~:text=This%20is%20the%20third%20installment,practices%20are%20vitally%20important%20to.
4. Dana Cuff, *Architectures of Spatial Justice* (MIT Press, 2023), 93.
5. Oliver Wainwright, "'Five Years to Do Ten Chuffing Houses!' Meet the Guerilla Gardeners of Granby," *The Guardian*, July 8, 2019, https://www.theguardian.com/artanddesign/2019/jul/08/assemble-guerrilla-gardeners-of-granby-liverpool-terrace-turner-prize.
6. Assemble Studio website, "Granby Four Streets" profile, https://assemblestudio.co.uk/projects/granby-four-streets-2.
7. Deborah Archer, transcribed from the video titled *The Architecture of Social Division* from the Aspen Ideas Festival 2024, https://www.aspenideas.org/sessions/the-architecture-of-social-division.
8. Jane Jacobs, "Can Big Plans Solve the Problem of Renewal?" Speech at the Residential Areas and Urban Renewal Conference, Hamburg, West Germany, October 12–14, 1981. As published in Samuel Zipp and Nathan Storring (eds.), *Vital Little Plans: The Short Works of Jane Jacobs* (Random House, 2016).
9. C. Larman and V. Basili, "Iterative and Incremental Development: A Brief History," *Computer* 36, no. 6 (2003): 47–56, doi:10.1109/MC.2003.1204375.
10. John F. C. Turner et al., "The Meaning of Autonomy," in *Freedom to Build* (MacMillan, 1972).
11. Cassim Shepard, "Housing Agency," *Places Journal*, November 2023, https://placesjournal.org/article/housing-legacies-of-john-turner/#:~:text=Turner%20is%20a%20study%20in%20apparent%20contradictions%3A%20an

%20anarchist%20distrustful,an%20architect%20who%20challenged %20the.

12. Clare Cumberlidge and Lucy Musgrave, *Design and Landscape for People: New Approaches for Renewal* (Thames and Hudson, 2007), 200.
13. Donald Watson, Alan Plattus, and Robert Shibley, *Time-Saver Standards for Urban Design* (McGraw-Hill, 2003), 4.11–6.
14. As quoted in Abhishek Pardeshi and Zarana Gandhi, "Critical Appraisal of Ideological Differences Between Patrick Geddes and Frederick Law Olmsted Theories of Urban Planning," *International Research Journal of Engineering and Technology* 6 (December 12, 2019).
15. Ibid.
16. Mike Lydon and Anthony Garcia, *Tactical Urbanism: Short-Term Action for Long-Term Change* (Island Press, 2015).
17. Author interview with Emmanuel Pratt, March 2024.
18. Maureen Feighan, "'Dot Project' to Put Heidelberg's Famous Dots Right on Street," *Detroit News*, July 26, 2022, https://www.detroitnews.com/story /entertainment/arts/2022/07/26/dot-project-bring-heidelbergs-trademark -polka-dots-detroit-street/10155311002/.
19. Oliver Wainwright, "The Street that Might Win the Turner Prize: How Assemble Are Transforming Toxteth," *The Guardian*, May 15, 2015, https: //www.theguardian.com/artanddesign/architecture-design-blog/2015 /may/12/assemble-turner-prize-2015-wildcard-how-the-young-architecture -crew-assemble-rocked-the-art-world.
20. Author interview with Susan Ross, March 2024.
21. Matteo Robiglio, *RE-USA: 20 American Stories of Adaptive Reuse, A Toolkit for Post-Industrial Cities* (jovis Verlag GmbH, 2017), 156.
22. "Since nonprofit organizations are not permitted to be architects of record in some states, they focus on design-related work that does not involve architectural services or the concomitant liability." Dana Cuff, *Architectures of Spatial Justice* (MIT Press, 2023), 56.
23. Ibid., 59.
24. American Institute of Architects, "Architect's Role in Creating Equitable Communities," September 2022, content.aia.org/sites/default/files/2022-09 /Architects_Role_in_Creating_Equitable_Communities.pdf.
25. ERA Architects website, "Tower Renewal" profile, https://www.eraarch.ca /projects/the-tower-renewal-project/.
26. Tower Renewal Project website, https://towerrenewal.com/.

27. Cynthia E. Smith, *Design for the Other 90%* (Smithsonian Cooper-Hewitt National Design Museum, 2007); and Cynthia E. Smith, *Design with the Other 90%: Cities* (Smithsonian Cooper-Hewitt National Design Museum, 2011).
28. The American Institute of Architects has published a guide to pro bono service activities. See https://content.aia.org/sites/default/files/2017-02/AIA-pro-bono-guidelines.pdf.
29. Susan Nigra Snyder, "On Preservation: Heritage, History, and Exclusion," *Architectural Record*, February 5, 2024.
30. Ibid.
31. Jacobs, "Can Big Plans Solve the Problem of Renewal?"
32. Nate Berg, "From Theaster Gates to Assemble: Is There an Art to Urban Regeneration?," *The Guardian*, November 3, 2015, https://www.theguardian.com/cities/2015/nov/03/theaster-gates-assemble-art-urban-regeneration-chicago.

CHAPTER 4

1. Maya Angelou, *Celebrations: Rituals of Peace and Prayer* (Random House New York, 2006).
2. Elin Kelsey, *Hope Matters: Why Changing the Way We Think Is Critical to Solving the Environmental Crisis* (Greystone Books, 2020).
3. Southwest Heritage Trust, "34540: Kilve Chantry, Kilve," Somerset Historic Environment Record, https://www.somersetheritage.org.uk/record/34540.
4. National Park Service, *Casa Grande Ruins: The History of Casa Grande Ruins National Monument*, http://npshistory.com/publications/cagr/history/sec7.htm#:~:text=On%20June%2028%2C%201902%20Congress.
5. Andrea Kalinová, "Off season: Documentary movie about Sanatorium Machnáč," 2018, https://abandonedrecreation.com/po-sezone/.
6. River Front Times, "Best Lost Cause: Mullanphy Emigrant Home," *Best of St. Louis 2007*, https://www.riverfronttimes.com/stlouis/best-lost-cause/BestOf?oid=2510046.
7. Michael R. Allen, "Mullanphy Emigrant Home, Four Years Later," Preservation Research Office, April 9, 2010, preservationresearch.com/historic-preservation/mullanphy-emigrant-home-four-years-later/
8. Chris Naffziger, "Mullanphy Emigrant Home: North St. Louis Landmark Slowly Returning to Glory," *Riverfront Times*, March 19, 2014, https://www

.riverfronttimes.com/newsblog/2014/03/19/mullanphy-emigrant-home-north-st-louis-landmark-slowly-returning-to-glory.

9. "The Mullanphy House—The New Building Nearly Completed," *Missouri Republican*, September 5, 1867.
10. Archive material made available by Old North St. Louis Restoration Group to author, November 2024.
11. "Mullanphy Historic District," *National Register of Historic Places Nomination Form*, 1982, https://mostateparks.com/sites/mostateparks/files/Mullanphy%20HD.pdf.
12. Jacob Barker, "New Owner of the Historic Mullanphy Emigrant Home Is a Modern-Day St. Louis Immigrant," *St. Louis Post Dispatch*, May 6, 2019, https://www.stltoday.com/business/local/new-owner-of-the-historic-mullanphy-emigrant-home-is-a/article_193df455-a278-55d9-a564-c8f3795afb59.html.
13. Author email correspondence with Michael Allen, March 2024.
14. Anna Powell-Smith, "Kilve" entry, Open Domesday, https://opendomesday.org/place/ST1442/kilve/.
15. English Heritage, *Heritage at Risk Register*, "Remains of Chantry at Kilve" entry, #1002960, https://historicengland.org.uk/advice/heritage-at-risk/search-register/list-entry/48507.
16. Enid Byford, *Somerset Curiosities* (Dovecote, 1989), 25.
17. English Heritage, *Heritage at Risk Register*, "Remains of Chantry at Kilve" entry, #1002960, and English Heritage, *Key to Terms and Abbreviations*, https://historicengland.org.uk/advice/heritage-at-risk/search-register/key-to-terms-and-abbreviations/.
18. Patrick Stow, email correspondence with author, March 2024.
19. Ibid.
20. Ibid.
21. Jacksonville (Florida) Zoning Code, https://library.municode.com/FL/Jacksonville/codes/Code_of_Ordinances?nodeId=TITVIICOHIPR_CH307HIPRPR_PT2APPR_S307.202ST.
22. Author email correspondence with Glora DeVall of Preservation SOS, November 2024.
23. Nicole Lopez, "Preservation Prevails," *Metro Jacksonville*, January 16, 2013, https://www.metrojacksonville.com/article/2013-jan-preservation-prevails-by-nicole-lopez.

24. Steve Patterson, Steve, "Mothballing of Crumbling Homes Could Save Jacksonville Homeowners," *The Florida Times-Union*, August 4, 2011, https://www.jacksonville.com/article/20110804/news/801246772.
25. Richard Cahan, *They All Fall Down: Richard Nickel's Struggle to Save America's Architecture* (John Wiley and Sons, 1994), 11.
26. City of Chicago, "Richard Nickel Studio," Landmark Designation Report, April 1, 2010, https://www.chicago.gov/content/dam/city/depts/zlup/Historic_Preservation/Publications/Richard_Nickel_Studio.pdf; Southern Illinois University Edwardsville, "Louis H. Sullivan Ornaments" page, https://collections.carli.illinois.edu/digital/collection/sie_arch.
27. After Nickel's death, his storefront studio eventually fell into foreclosure and disrepair and was threatened with demolition in 2008. In 2009, the Chicago Landmarks Commission voted to recommend the historic designation of the Richard Nickel Studio.
28. "Where there's a strong market for salvaged architectural items, it can encourage the demolition of significant buildings or the alteration of significant buildings," says Vince Michael, former director of Chicago programs for the Landmarks Preservation Council of Illinois, in J. R. Jones, "Salvage Love," *The Chicago Reader*, May 15, 1997, https://chicagoreader.com/news-politics/salvage-love/.
29. For a brief overview, see Amy Hetletvedt, "Beyond Sustainability: Exploring the Ethics of Architectural Salvage," *Arcade Magazine* 33, no. 3 (April 2016).
30. The entire trading room has been reconstructed inside the Art Institute of Chicago, and the provenance line in the museum's catalog reads "Gift of the Three Oaks Wrecking Company." "Chicago Stock Exchange Trading Room: Reconstruction at the Art Institute of Chicago" entry, https://www.artic.edu/artworks/156538/chicago-stock-exchange-trading-room-reconstruction-at-the-art-institute-of-chicago.
31. As quoted in David Uberti, "Story of Cities #45: The Death of Richard Nickel, Guardian of Chicago's Heritage," *The Guardian*, May 18, 2016, https://www.theguardian.com/cities/2016/may/18/story-cities-death-richard-nickel-guardian-chicago-heritage-architecture.
32. US Library of Congress, "Background and Scope of the Collections," *Historic American Buildings Survey/Historic American Engineering Record/Historic American Landscapes Survey*, https://www.loc.gov/pictures/collection/hh/background.html.

33. For a brief overview, see Diana Craig Patch, "A Monumental Gift to the Met," The Metropolitan Museum of Art, New York, https://www.metmuseum.org/about-the-met/collection-areas/egyptian-art/temple-of-dendur-50/gift-to-the-met.
34. Ada Louise Huxtable, *Goodbye History, Hello Hamburger: An Anthology of Architectural Delights and Disasters* (Preservation Press, 1986).
35. Ada Louise Huxtable, "Where Did We Go Wrong?," *The New York Times*, July 14, 1968, in Ada Louise Huxtable, *Goodbye History, Hello Hamburger: An Anthology of Architectural Delights and Disasters* (Preservation Press, 1986).
36. Richard Macias, "Moving Houses: A Strategy for Urban Neighborhood Reuse," in Richard L. Austin, *Adaptive Reuse: Issues and Case Studies in Building Preservation* (Van Nostrand Reinhold, 1988).
37. "Relocation and dismantling of an existing resource should be employed only as a last resort, if protection cannot be achieved by any other means." ICOMOS Appleton Charter, 1983, https://www.icomos.org/images/DOCUMENTS/Charters/appleton.pdf.
38. James H. Andrews in Christine Kukka, "Relocating Old Houses: Saving or Losing History?," *New York Times*, June 30, 1991.

CHAPTER 5

1. Grace Ong Yan, "The Infinite Spontaneity of Tradition," Pritzker Prize essay 2012, https://www.pritzkerprize.com/2012/essay.
2. Emily P. Freeman, *A Million Little Ways: Uncover the Art You Were Made to Live* (Revell, 2013).
3. *New York Times Magazine* writer M. H. Miller states, "Guyton was one of the first artists anywhere to try to use art to materially improve a community, long before this became a contemporary cliché." See M. H. Miller, "Tyree Guyton Turned a Detroit Street into a Museum. Why Is He Taking It Down?," *New York Times Magazine*, May 9, 2019, https://www.nytimes.com/2019/05/09/magazine/tyree-guyton-art-detroit.html.
4. Tyree Guyton, in *Connecting the Dots: Tyree Guyton's Heidelberg Project* (Wayne State University Press, 2007), vii.
5. John Gallagher, *Reimagining Detroit: Opportunities for Redefining an American City* (Wayne State University Press, 2010).
6. Louis Aguilar, "Twelve Heidelberg Fires, All a Mystery," *The Detroit News*, February 20, 2015, https://www.detroitnews.com/story/news/special-reports/2015/02/20/heidelberg-arsons-detroit-hard-solve/23769375/.

7. The Heidelberg Project website, "History," https://www.heidelberg.org/history.
8. Jenenne Whitfield, in *Connecting the Dots: Tyree Guyton's Heidelberg Project* (Wayne State University Press, 2007), 127.
9. Heidelberg Project website, "Our Next Chapter," https://www.heidelberg.org/our-future-by-the-numbers.
10. Author email correspondence with Jenenne Whitfield, December 2024.
11. Andrew Herscher, "Detroit Art City: Urban Decline, Aesthetic Production, Public Interest," in Margaret Dewar and June Manning Thomas (eds.), *The City After Abandonment* (University of Pennsylvania Press, 2013), 69.
12. Ibid, 73.
13. Heather Hall and Rose Olfert, "Saskatchewan," Government of Canada State of Rural Canada (undated), https://sorc.crrf.ca/saskatchewan/.
14. Andrew Markle, "What's Left Behind," *Galleries West*, April 30, 2009, https://www.gallerieswest.ca/magazine/stories/what%E2%80%99s-left-behind/.
15. Heather Benning website, "Marysburg Project," http://www.heatherbenning.ca/the-marysburg-project.html (profile no longer accessible).
16. Author email correspondence with Heather Benning, April 2024.
17. Ibid.
18. Heather Benning website, "Dollhouse," https://heatherbenning.ca/dollhouse/.
19. Emily Flitter, "Insurer's Retreat in Florida Signals Crisis with No Easy Fix," *The New York Times*, July 14, 2023, https://www.nytimes.com/2023/07/14/business/farmers-homeowners-insurance-florida.html.
20. As pointed out in a *New York Times* article about Mrs. Bryant's death (which occurred during the writing of this book), the only two people who knew precisely what happened that day were Emmett Till and Mrs. Bryant. Margalit Fox, "Carolyn Bryant Donham Dies at 88. Her Words Doomed Emmett Till," *New York Times*, April 27, 2023, https://www.nytimes.com/2023/04/27/us/carolyn-bryant-donham-dead.html.
21. Maureen Corrigan, "Let the People See: It Took Courage to Keep Emmett Till's Memory Alive," book review of *Let the People See* by Elliott J. Gorn, National Public Radio, October 30, 2018, https://www.npr.org/2018/10/30/660980178/-let-the-people-see-shows-how-emmett-till-s-murder-was-nearly-forgotten.
22. Audra D. S. Burch, Veda Shastri, and Tim Chaffee, "Emmett Till's Murder, and How America Remembers Its Darkest Moments," *New York Times*, February 20, 2019, https://www.nytimes.com/interactive/2019/02/20/us/emmett-till-murder-legacy.html.

23. Dave Tell, "Remembering Emmett Till in Money, Mississippi," *Places Journal*, April 2019, https://placesjournal.org/article/remembering-emmett-till/?cn-reloaded=1.
24. English Heritage, "Church of St. Luke" entry, #1280622, https://historicengland.org.uk/listing/the-list/list-entry/1280622.
25. Gabriel Moshenka provides a review of the types of curated memorials and their collective functions. See Gabriel Moshenska, "Curated Ruins and the Endurance of Conflict Heritage," *Conservation and Management of Archaeological Sites* 17, no. 1 (2015): 77–90, doi:10.1179/1350503315Z.00000000095.
26. St Luke's Bombed Out Church website. "The Story: A Testament to Community Spirit," https://www.slboc.com/the-story.
27. Azra Aksamija, Raafat Majzoub, and Melina Pilippou (eds.), *Design to Live: Everyday Inventions from a Refugee Camp* (MIT Press, 2021). Also profiled in Greta Rainbow, "'Existing Is an Act of Resistance': The Syrian Refugees Creating Design from Displacement," *The Guardian*, October 18, 2021, https://www.theguardian.com/artanddesign/2021/oct/18/syrian-refugees-venice-architecture-biennale.
28. Sarah Rose Sharp, "Restoring Memories and Forging Futures with Carl Nielbock of CAN Art Handworks," *ModelD*, September 5, 2016, https://www.modeldmedia.com/features/can-art-handworks-050916.aspx.
29. Ibid.
30. Carlos Nielbock, transcribed from the film *Clock Tower Project* on the website https://www.canarthandworks.com.
31. William Allison Bostick, *Public Execution*, 1961. Collage, ink, and oil on paper. In the collection of the Detroit Institute of Arts, https://dia.org/collection/public-execution-35148.

CHAPTER 6

1. Rupert Neate, "Scandal of Europe's 11m Empty Homes," *The Guardian*, February 23, 2014, https://www.theguardian.com/society/2014/feb/23/europe-11m-empty-properties-enough-house-homeless-continent-twice.
2. Local Government Ireland website, page for "Offer a Home," https://offerahome.ie/?faq=1.
3. Carla Bruni, "Vacant Buildings for Refugees: A Case Study in the Power of Adaptive Reuse of Older and Historic Buildings for Resilience," *World Heritage USA*, https://worldheritageusa.org/vacant-buildings-for-refugees

-a-case-study-in-the-power-of-adaptive-reuse-of-older-and-historic-buildings-for-resilience/.

4. Author email correspondence with Erica Wiley, development director for WELD Seattle, December 2024.
5. Ibid.
6. See, for example, the EU "Refill" project report, summarizing how reuse of vacant space spurred innovation at the local level, https://urbact.eu/sites/default/files/2023-04/refill_final_publication.pdf.
7. Matteo Robiglio, *RE-USA: 20 American Stories of Adaptive Reuse, A Toolkit for Post-Industrial Cities* (jovis Verlag GmbH, 2017), 157.
8. As quoted in Laura Latham, "The Rise of the 'Meanwhile Space': How Empty Properties Are Finding Second Lives," *The Guardian*, November 28, 2018, https://www.theguardian.com/cities/2018/nov/28/the-rise-of-the-meanwhile-space-how-empty-properties-are-finding-second-lives.
9. Development Trusts Association & Meanwhile Space CIC, "*No Time to Waste. . . . The Meanwhile Use of Assets for Community Benefit*," May 2010.
10. Lewis Carroll, *Through the Looking Glass* (MacMillan, 1872).
11. Les Grands Voisins, https://lesgrandsvoisins.org/.
12. Les Grands Voisins, https://lesgrandsvoisins.org/2019/04/11/un-frigo-solidaire-cour-robin/.
13. Paris et Métropole Aménagement, *St. Vincent de Paul: Another Kind of Paris*, 2023, https://www.parisetmetropole-amenagement.fr/sites/default/files/2023-03/230316%20PLAQUETTE%20SVP-WEB-EN-DEF.pdf.
14. Ibid., 29.
15. Ibid., 6.
16. Michael Bohn, "Sometimes, the Better Alternative Is Not to Build New Things," *Common Edge*, October 25, 2022, https://commonedge.org/sometimes-the-better-alternative-is-not-to-build-new-things/.
17. Ferdinando Cotungo, "Italian Renaissance," *Smithsonian Magazine*, April/May 2022, citing statistics from the National Association of Italian Municipalities (ANCI).
18. Catherine Slessor, "Million Donkey Hotel by feld72, Prata Sannita, Italy," *Architectural Review*, December 1, 2009, https://www.architectural-review.com/awards/ar-emerging-architecture/million-donkey-hotel-by-feld72-prata-sannita-italy.
19. Author email correspondence with feld72, December 2024.

20. *Million Donkey Hotel*, http://www.feld72.at/en/?s=million+donkey#/.
21. Amy Kolczak, "Historic Retreats: The Inn on Ferry Street," *Old House Online*, June 17, 2021, https://www.oldhouseonline.com/house-tours/historic-retreats-the-inn-on-ferry-street/#:~:text=The%2040%2Droom%20hotel%20opened,fantastic%20architecture%2C%E2%80%9D%20Mosey%20says.
22. Michigan Urban Farming Initiative website, "Urban Farm to Convert Blighted Home into Cistern and Outdoor Community Space," https://www.miufi.org/blighted-home-transformed-into-cist.
23. Elizabeth Yarina, "Repurposed Vertical Farms: Adaptive Building Reuse for Vertical Urban Agriculture," *MIT Urban Nature and City Design*, student paper, Fall 2012, https://web.mit.edu/nature/projects_12/eliz.html.
24. Michael Deibert, "Resurrecting Newburgh, the Once-Grand American City that Had Its Heart Torn Out," *The Guardian*, April 8, 2015, https://www.theguardian.com/cities/2015/apr/08/resurrecting-newburgh-once-grand-american-city-heart-torn-out.
25. Mary McTamaney, "Exploring the Skeleton of a Classic Structure," *Mid-Hudson Times*, August 5, 2021, https://www.timeshudsonvalley.com/mid-hudson-times/stories/exploring-the-skeleton-of-a-classic-structure,30471.
26. Sidney K. Robinson, "The Picturesque: Sinister Dishevelment," in Marco Diani and Catherine Ingraham (eds.), *Restructuring Architectural Theory* (Rizzoli, 1988), 74–9.
27. Author email correspondence with Kelly Schroer, November 2024.
28. Malea Martin, "A Historic Phoenix Church Overtaken by Nature Finds New Life," *Preservation Magazine*, Fall 2024, https://savingplaces.org/stories/a-historic-phoenix-church-overtaken-by-nature-finds-new-life.
29. De Ceuvel website, https://deceuvel.nl/en/about/general-information/.
30. Benjamin Chavis Jr. and Charles Lee, "Toxic Wastes and Race in the United States: A National Report on the Racial and Socio-economic Characteristics of Communities with Hazardous Waste Sites," Commission for Racial Justice—United Church of Christ, 1987, https://new.uccfiles.com/pdf/ToxicWastes&Race.pdf.
31. Dorceta E. Taylor, *Toxic Communities: Environmental Racism, Industrial Pollution, and Residential Mobility*, (New York University Press, 2014).
32. Art21 interview with Mel Chin (undated), https://art21.org/read/mel-chin-revival-field/.

33. Transylvania Trust, "Bánffy Castle" entry, http://www.transylvaniatrust.ro/en/banffy-castle/.
34. "History of Bánffy Castle from Bonțida" entry on the Built Heritage Conservation site, http://www.heritagetraining-banffycastle.org/index.php/en/banffy-castle-bontida/history.
35. Author email correspondence with Zsuzsanna Eke, March 2024.
36. Transylvania Trust, "Restoration of Banffy Castle" entry https://www.transylvaniatrust.ro/en/program/the-restoration-of-banffy-castle-bontida/.
37. For a good overview, see Vicky Gan, "How the City of Mud Stays Standing: Meet the Masons of Djenné, Mali," *Smithsonian Magazine*, September 30, 2013, https://www.smithsonianmag.com/smithsonian-institution/how-the-city-of-mud-stays-standing-meet-the-masons-of-djenne-mali-224225/.
38. Dan Rooney and Carol Peterson, *Allegheny City: A History of Pittsburgh's North Side* (University of Pittsburgh Press, 2013), 92.
39. Ibid., 220.
40. Phone interview with John Martine, retired architect, 2016. Martine participated in the project while a principal architect at IAS. Author email correspondence with John Martine, December 2024.
41. Author email correspondence with Rachel Callison, daughter of Mary Callison, first homeowner of Denny Row rehabilitation project, 2024.
42. John Martine, "Denny Row" project profile, prepared while working at IAS, Pittsburgh, provided by John Martine to author.

CHAPTER 7

1. Theaster Gates, transcribed from *Theaster Gates: Soul Food Pavilion* video produced by University of Chicago Smart Museum of Art, 2012, https://www.youtube.com/watch?v=king4z1kTKI.
2. University of Chicago Smart Museum of Art Exhibit, *Feast: Radical Hospitality in Contemporary Art*, February 16–June 10, 2012, https://smartmuseum.uchicago.edu/exhibitions/feast/.
3. Maria Fee, *Beauty Is a Basic Service: Theology and Hospitality in the Work of Theaster Gates* (Fortress Press, 2023), 6.
4. Theaster Gates, transcribed from University of Chicago Smart Museum of Art video "On Hospitality," 2012, https://vimeo.com/41539242.
5. Lauren Walser, "Theaster Gates, Jr. Is Restoring His Community, One House at a Time," *Preservation*, Spring 2012.

6. Fee, *Beauty Is a Basic Service*, 3. Ben Austen, "Chicago's Opportunity Artist," *New York Times Magazine*, December 20, 2013, https://www.nytimes.com/2013/12/22/magazine/chicagos-opportunity-artist.html.
7. Orhan Pamuk, *The Innocence of Objects* (Abrams, 2012).
8. John Colapinto, "Letter from Chicago: The Real-Estate Artist," *The New Yorker*, January 12, 2014.
9. Maria Fee, *Beauty Is a Basic Service: Theology and Hospitality in the Work of Theaster Gates* (Fortress Press, 2023), 4.
10. Theaster Gates website, "12 Ballads for Huguenot House," https://www.theastergates.com/exhibitions/12-ballads-for-huguenot-house.
11. Colapinto, "Letter from Chicago."
12. See also Amy Hetletvedt, "Beyond Sustainability: Exploring the Ethics of Architectural Salvage," *Arcade Magazine* 33, no. 3 (2016).
13. Ben Austen, "Chicago's Opportunity Artist."
14. Ibid.
15. Josephine Minutillo, "Newsmaker: Theaster Gates," *Architectural Record*, April 30, 2014, https://www.architecturalrecord.com/articles/3129-newsmaker-theaster-gates.
16. Ibid.
17. Colapinto, "Letter from Chicago."
18. As cited in Heather McGhee's book *The Sum of Us*, a 2017 report by the Federal Reserve Bank of Chicago traced the areas redlined in 1930s lending maps to a racial gap in homeownership (and thus wealth) up to fifty years later. See Heather, McGhee, *The Sum of Us: What Racism Costs Everyone and How We Can Prosper Together* (One World, 2021), 368.
19. Minutillo, "Newsmaker: Theaster Gates."
20. Tim Adams, "Chicago Artist Theaster Gates: I'm Hoping Swiss Bankers Will Bail Out My Flooded South Side Bank in the Name of Art," *The Guardian*, May 3, 2015, https://www.theguardian.com/artanddesign/2015/may/03/theaster-gates-artist-chicago-dorchester-projects.
21. Gates as quoted in Walser, "Theaster Gates, Jr. Is Restoring His Community."
22. Adams, "Chicago Artist Theaster Gates."
23. Richard McCoy, "Exploring the Freedom to Re-Present Value. A Discussion with Theaster Gates," *Art21* magazine, April 19, 2011, https://magazine.art21.org/2011/04/19/no-preservatives-exploring-the-freedom-to-re-present-value-a-discussion-with-theaster-gates/.

CHAPTER 8

1. Michael J. Lewis, "Neither Ruin nor Replica: The Restoration of Virginia's Menokin Plantation House Takes a Sophisticated, Ambitious Approach to Historic Preservation," *The Wall Street Journal*, October 28, 2020, https://www.wsj.com/articles/neither-ruin-nor-replica-11603912321.
2. Menokin Foundation website, "The Story of the House," https://www.menokin.org/story-of-the-house.
3. Architect Amber Wiley has suggested that HABS, in particular, could be part of a reinvigorated Works Progress Administration (WPA): "An expanded HABS program that draws on underemployed designers, preservationists, and humanities graduates could easily fit under the umbrella of a modern-day WPA." See Amber Wiley, "A Modern-Day WPA," in Max Page and Marla R. Miller (eds.), *Bending the Future: 50 Ideas for the Next 50 Years of Historic Preservation in the United States* (University of Massachusetts Press, 2016).
4. Michelle Smith, "How Wood Became Menokin's Savior," *Northern Neck News*, December 7, 2022, https://static1.squarespace.com/static/5f0dc027e6ecb31d198aedd3/t/63b4889ee9f62d72cfde34e7/1672775844434/Menokin+Woodwork+NNN.pdf.
5. The landmark status was acquired in 1971. See https://www.nps.gov/subjects/nationalhistoriclandmarks/list-of-nhls-by-state.htm#onthisPage-46.
6. Menokin Foundation website, "The Structure over Menokin," https://www.menokin.org/digital-content/the-structure-over-menokin.
7. Meghan O'Connor, "18th Century House Ruin to Be Restored . . . with Glass," *National Trust for Historic Preservation*, December 3, 2014, https://savingplaces.org/stories/menokin-foundation-restored-structural-glass.
8. Lewis, "Neither Ruin nor Replica."
9. Menokin Foundation website, "The Glass House Project," https://www.menokin.org/the-glass-house-project.
10. Lewis, "Neither Ruin nor Replica."
11. The Menokin Foundation, transcribed from the video "In the Glass with Menokin: The Remembrance Structure," https://www.menokin.org/remembrance-structure.
12. Ibid.
13. Author interview with Calder Loth, March 2024.

14. Menokin Foundation website, "The Story of the Land," https://www.menokin.org/story-of-the-land.
15. Author interview with Reid Freeman, March 2024.
16. Website of Witherford Watson Mann Architects, "Astley," http://www.wwmarchitects.co.uk/projects/astley.
17. Smith, "How Wood Became Menokin's Savior."
18. Lewis, "Neither Ruin nor Replica."

CHAPTER 9

1. BBC, "*Toxteth Riots*" (25th anniversary piece), July 28, 2006, http://www.bbc.co.uk/liverpool/content/articles/2006/06/28/toxteth_anniversary_feature.shtml.
2. Demolitions were taking place through Compulsory Purchase Orders (CPOs), which function somewhat like eminent domain in the United States. Granby residents won a successful Public Inquiry of the CPO, battling against continued demolition. As described in Jonathan Brown, "Why Were the Four Streets Emptied Out Anyway? A Granby Back Story," in *Granby Workshop Catalogue 2015*, published by the Granby Workshop.
3. Leroy Cooper, as quoted in "Leroy Cooper, Toxteth 1980s," *British Culture Archive*, https://britishculturearchive.co.uk/leroy-cooper-toxteth-1980s/.
4. Nate Berg, "From Theaster Gates to Assemble: Is There an Art to Urban Regeneration?," *The Guardian*, November 3, 2015, https://www.theguardian.com/cities/2015/nov/03/theaster-gates-assemble-art-urban-regeneration-chicago.
5. Author interview with Hazel Tilley, April 2024.
6. Assemble Studio website, "Granby Winter Garden," https://assemblestudio.co.uk/projects/granby-winter-gardens. Transcribed from the film "Granby Winter Garden 360°," a collaboration between Rob Vincent, Popla Media, and Assemble.
7. Hazel Tilley, in "'You'd Lie There in the Night and Hear a Piece of Wood Go.' Transcription of a Conversation with Hazel Tilley on the Granby Residents Association and Beyond," in *Granby Workshop Catalogue 2015*, published by the Granby Workshop.
8. Granby Four Streets CLT website, https://www.granby4streetsclt.co.uk/history-of-the-four-streets.
9. Ibid.

10. Community Land Trust Network website, https://www.communitylandtrusts.org.uk/about-clts/what-is-a-community-land-trust-clt/.
11. Power to Change website, "Granby Four Streets," https://www.powertochange.org.uk/case_study/granby-four-streets/.
12. Ian Youngs, "Liverpool's Turner Prize Houses Sold with 'Anti-Gentrification' Clause," *BBC News*, December 5, 2016, https://www.bbc.com/news/entertainment-arts-38194911#:~:text=The%20first%20houses%20to%20be,derelict%20houses%20in%20Toxteth%2C%20Liverpool.
13. Oliver Wainwright, "The Street that Might Win the Turner Prize: How Assemble Are Transforming Toxteth," *The Guardian*, May 15, 2015, https://www.theguardian.com/artanddesign/architecture-design-blog/2015/may/12/assemble-turner-prize-2015-wildcard-how-the-young-architecture-crew-assemble-rocked-the-art-world.
14. Assemble Studio website, "Granby Four Streets," https://assemblestudio.co.uk/projects/granby-four-streets-2.
15. *Granby Workshop Catalogue 2015*, published by the Granby Workshop.
16. Oliver Wainwright, "'Five Years to Do Ten Chuffing Houses!' Meet the Guerilla Gardeners of Granby," *The Guardian*, July 8, 2019, https://www.theguardian.com/artanddesign/2019/jul/08/assemble-guerrilla-gardeners-of-granby-liverpool-terrace-turner-prize.
17. Assemble Studio website, "Granby Winter Garden," https://assemblestudio.co.uk/projects/granby-winter-gardens, including the film "Granby Winter Garden 360°," a collaboration between Rob Vincent, Popla Media, and Assemble.
18. Ibid. Transcribed from the film "Granby Winter Garden 360°."
19. Granby 4 Streets Community Land Trust website, "Granby Winter Garden," https://www.granby4streetsclt.co.uk/granby-winter-garden.

CHAPTER 10

1. Rick Lowe, transcribed from video of Rick Lowe's 2015 Class Day lecture at the Harvard Graduate School of Design, https://www.ricklowe.com/timeline.html.
2. Michael Kimmelman, "In Houston, Art Is Where the Home Is," *New York Times*, December 17, 2006, http://www.nytimes.com/2006/12/17/arts/design/17kimm.html?pagewanted=all&_r=0.

3. For an introductory history, see Charlette Caldwell, "The Lowliest Type?: The Historiography of the Shotgun House," *The Avery Review* 37(February 2019). A project of the Office of Publications at the Columbia University Graduate School of Architecture, Planning, and Preservation, https://averyreview.com/issues/37/lowliest-type.
4. Lowe, transcribed from video of Rick Lowe's 2015 Class Day lecture.
5. These antecedents for the shotgun house are described in the *Field Guide to American Houses*: "Some scholars note that similar forms are common in the West Indies and trace them from Africa to early Haitian influences in New Orleans, whence they became popular with Black freedman migrating to southern urban centers following the Civil War." Virginia and Lee McAlester, *A Field Guide to American Houses* (Knopf, 1984), 90.
6. Lowe, transcribed from video of Rick Lowe's 2015 Class Day lecture.
7. Project Row Houses website, "History," https://projectrowhouses.org/about/history/.
8. Ibid.
9. Clare Cumberlidge and Lucy Musgrave, *Design and Landscape for People: New Approaches to Renewal* (Thames and Hudson, 2007), 198.
10. Author interview with Rick Lowe, December 2024.
11. In Houston's Fourth Ward, Freedman's Town was one of the communities sliced through by a freeway project (I-45), like those mentioned in the Introduction. See Andrea Roberts, "The End of Bootstraps and Good Masters: Fostering Social Inclusion by Creating Counternarratives," in Erica Avrami, *Issues in Preservation Policy: Preservation and Social Inclusion* (Columbia Books on Architecture and the City, 2020).
12. Dennis Ryan, "Artists in Action," in *Collective Creative Actions: Project Row Houses at 25* (Duke University Press, 2018).
13. Helen Pidd, "Greenpeace Activists Arrested After Ending Oil Protest at Sunak's Mansion," *The Guardian*, August 3, 2023, https://www.theguardian.com/politics/2023/aug/03/greenpeace-protesters-drape-giant-oil-black-fabric-over-sunaks-mansion.
14. Kimmelman, "In Houston, Art Is Where the Home Is."
15. George Lipsitz, "Neighborhood Development and Art-Based Community Making," in *Collective Creative Actions: Project Row Houses at 25* (Duke University Press, 2018).

16. US Department of Housing and Urban Development, Office of Policy of Development and Research, case study on Project Row Houses, https: //www.huduser.gov/portal/casestudies/study-062421.html.
17. Assata-Nicole Richards, "A Soft Place to Stand: Escaping the Interlocking Systems of Race, Class, and Gender," in *Collective Creative Actions: Project Row Houses at 25* (Duke University Press, 2018).

CONCLUSION

1. Dana Cuff, *Architectures of Spatial Justice* (The MIT Press, 2023).
2. Donald Miller, *A Million Miles in a Thousand Years: What I Learned While Editing My Life* (Thomas Nelson, 2009).

Acknowledgments

> "If you find a book you really want to read but it hasn't been written yet, then you must write it."
>
> —Toni Morrison, 1981 speech to Ohio Arts Council

Every project needs cheerleaders and challengers, and the occasional person who can be both. Among this group for me are Rachel Birch, Janai Gilmore, Jane O'Sullivan, and Amy Sullivan. Thanks to Grant Hildebrand for strategic guidance and lending courage; to Phil Davis for the opportunity to talk publicly about my work at an early stage; to my praying friends Lisa Cannata, Bea Chen, Lisa Dickey, Kelly Ortell, and especially Denisha Mathews, who prayed for me from the window across the street for several years as I was writing it.

I'm grateful for the community and camaraderie of women architect friends around the world: Changfang, Akuto, Miša, Eva, Hana, Laura, Sihem, Wafa, Raja, Fatma, and Sonia; for Dr. Sharon Sutton, FAIA, who has been a mentor for three decades of my academic and professional life; for employers and colleagues in Chicago, Seattle, and Detroit who invested in my early professional journey and taught me to ask good questions; and for adventurous people in my life who have been examples of loving buildings and communities in tangible ways, including Flora Bennett, Brian and Megan Meyers, and Dan and Lisa Johanon.

Thanks to those involved with the case studies who dedicated time for interviews and reviewed text about the projects: Michael Allen, Nicolas Aubin, Danielle Burns Wilson, Rachel Callison, Andrew Daley, Gloria DeVall, Zsuzsanna Eke, Reid Freeman, John George, Courtney Hug, Jason Jackson, Andrea Kalinová, Jia Lok Pratt, Calder Loth, Rick Lowe, John Martine, Emmanuel Pratt, Kelly Schroer, Patrick Stow, Hazel Tilley, Jenenne Whitfield, and Martin Zaiček; to Mick McCulloch, Jessica Puff, Virginia Price, and Susan Ross, who read and provided valuable feedback on portions of the manuscript; to Carol Highsmith, who donated a lifetime collection of her architectural photos to the Library of Congress and put them in the public domain; to the IFDA Education Foundation and the James Marston Fitch Charitable Foundation for their support of the publication and the Michigan Architectural Foundation Damian Farrell Awareness Grant for support to share its message; and to the fifty people who donated to the campaign to help print this book in full-color splendor. Here it is!

Thanks to the team at Island Press for believing in *Preserving with Purpose*, especially my editor, Heather Boyer, who saw the potential and spent many hours helping shape the final product.

Thanks to my family for providing life perspective and humor at critical points; to my parents for encouraging a child they didn't always understand; to my sister and brother-in-law, dream enablers, whose sense of humor and levity are unmatched; to my husband, Andrew, who has supported my career and my sanity since the days he helped me solder models together in architecture school; and to my children for the reality checks of well-timed, sarcastic ridicule. It's a love language.

Big idea projects are never finished. Thanks for walking alongside me through the middle.

About the Author

Amy Hetletvedt is a licensed architect, preservationist, and educator who has been supporting buildings, the people who love them, and the communities they serve for more than twenty years. She has lived on four continents, collaborating on projects in a variety of scales and settings.

Hetletvedt has served on the Historic District Commission for the City of Detroit and has taught design studios and architectural ethics. Her writing has appeared in *ArchDaily*, *Slate*, *Docomomo*, and regional architectural media.

Hetletvedt holds a BS Arch from the University of Michigan and a Master of Architecture from the University of Washington.

Out of the cacophony of critics and experts in our noisy world, Hetletvedt contributes a warm and authentic voice, walking alongside others in conversation about complex but essential questions.

She can be reached at amyhetletvedt.com.

J Photography of Grand Rapids